Quarterly Essay

CONTENTS

Quarterly Essay is published four times a year by Black Inc., an imprint of Schwartz Publishing Pty Ltd
Publisher: Morry Schwartz

ISBN 1 86395 386 8

Subscriptions (4 issues): $34.95 a year within Australia incl. GST (Institutional subs. $40). Outside Australia $70. Payment may be made by Mastercard, Visa or Bankcard, or by cheque made out to Schwartz Publishing. Payment includes postage and handling.

Correspondence and subscriptions should be addressed to the Editor at:
Schwartz Publishing.
Level 3, 167 Collins St
Melbourne VIC 3000
Australia
Phone: 61 3 9654 2000
Fax: 61 3 9654 2290
Email: quarterlyessay@blackincbooks.com

Editor: Peter Craven
Management: Silvia Kwon
Assistant Editor: Chris Feik
Publishing Assistant: Sophy Williams
Design: Guy Mirabella

Quarterly Essay aims to present significant contributions to political, intellectual and cultural debate. It is a magazine in extended pamphlet form and by publishing in each issue a single writer of at least 20,000 words we hope to mediate between the limitations of the newspaper column, where there is the danger that evidence and argument can be swallowed up by the form, and the kind of full-length study of a subject where the only readership is a necessarily specialised one. *Quarterly Essay* aims for the attention of the committed general reader. Although it is a periodical which wants subscribers, each number of the journal will be the length of a short book because we want our writers to have the opportunity to speak to the broadest possible audience without condescension or populist shortcuts. *Quarterly Essay* wants to get away from the tyranny that space limits impose in contemporary journalism and we will be giving our essayists the space to express the evidence for their views and those who disagree with them the chance to reply at whatever length is necessary. *Quarterly Essay* will not be confined to politics but it will be centrally concerned with it. We are not interested in occupying any particular point on the political map and we hope to bring our readership the widest range of political and cultural opinion which is compatible with truth-telling, style and command of the essay form.

INTRODUCTION

John Birmingham's *Appeasing Jakarta* is an attempt to come to terms with Australia's dealings with East Timor and an attempt to use this as a window on what might be possible in our dealings with our large and turbulent neighbour.

It is the story of how Australian politicians and bureaucrats – in the first instance Gough Whitlam and Richard Woolcott – accepted the idea of the Indonesian takeover of East Timor and how this proved to be such a disastrous policy, not primarily because it was cynical, but because it showed such naïveté about what was possible in the relationship between a pluralist democracy like Australia and a dictatorship like Indonesia. There was also a naïveté, John Birmingham believes, in not realising that Indonesian annexation of East Timor was likely to provoke the very nationalism it was meant to quell.

Appeasing Jakarta is an analysis of what happened in 1975 when we condoned Indonesia's intervention, and of what happened in 1999 when we stood against it. It is an essay which takes a cold-eyed look at what politicians and diplomats will do when they think they have a grasp of *realpolitik* and the national interest but it is also, by design and with great sweep and passion, an essay about the human cost: about the blood and terror that comes when a corrupt regime behaves as you would expect and the powermen of an opposite society reserve their depths of understanding for the oppressors rather than the oppressed.

Appeasing Jakarta is, in part, a powerful narrative full of the smell of blood and the shrieks of lamentation. For long sections it tells the story of what happened on the ground in East Timor to the people who were beaten into it. It is written with great energy by a man who is appalled at the human detail of what was violated in East Timor but who – for that very reason – brings to its depiction a scathing dispassion and a scorn that is not separate from his sense of sorrow and pity. This is an essay by a writer who is discernibly exercised by the mechanisms of war and alive to its excitements, a man who seems to understand what Robert E. Lee meant when he said, 'It is well war is so terrible or else we would grow too fond of it.' But he is also a writer who refuses to see a problem in foreign relations in anything but human terms. Not that he wishes to sentimentalise the problem: his primary objection to the Whitlams and Woolcotts is that he thinks they had no grasp of the national interest in this matter.

John Birmingham has plenty of admiration for the restraint and discipline of the young men and women who went into East Timor in 1999 under Peter Cosgrove, and there is also a quality of mercy which he brings to the various political figures he feels that he must, to a greater or lesser extent, arraign. In this respect it's remarkable that he manages to find a good word or two for both Paul Keating and John Howard – scarcely sympathetic figures to him – the belated masters of 'engagement' and 'divorce' in the matter of Indonesia. He acknowledges the cost of Keating's (and Evans') rapprochement with Indonesia but refuses to deny its sanity or its savvy. He is withering about the naïveté of the Howard Government in the lead-up to the 1999 independence referendum (in various ways duplicating the follies of the Whitlam Government a generation earlier) but he is,

in his understated way, admiring of the fact that John Howard was prepared for war when the crunch came.

This is an essay written in flowing colours with a strong narrative
streak and a swashbuckling power of dispatch. It is a work by a man who
became famous for *He Died with a Felafel in his Hand*, that documentary com-
edy of communal living (now a film) and who went on to become the
most notable 'new journalist' we have, notating the complex charisma of
Pauline Hanson and writing a history of Sydney so black that the
revenants of the Rum Corps seem to rise spectre-like from its pages.

But if John Birmingham is a gonzo, he is a gonzo who rides into battle
out of something more than the lust for savagery and the Technicolor orna-
mentation of blood and guts. *Appeasing Jakarta* is a miniature narrative history
of this nation's complicity in East Timor which is the opposite of naive
even though John Birmingham makes the deliberate decision to juxtapose
the delineation of policy (so elegant and dissectible) with the animated
agonies of the people of East Timor, the images of death and pain and
deformation unforgettably shadowing the apprehension of how a mistake
of judgement in foreign policy could be repeated over and over again.

John Birmingham is deadly in his disdain for the way a defunct paradigm that had long proved its futility was clung to like a dogma by men
of great intelligence and self-conscious worldliness who should have
known better. And at the same time (because he is always tender-mind-
ed in the end) he stresses the articulateness and the foresight of the voices
(in Foreign Affairs, in government) who said otherwise.

This is a pamphlet full of an implicit sense of the power and the glory
of pluralist democracy, even in Australia, even in the context of the sorry
history of how government and bureaucracy, the Prime Ministers and
mandarins, behaved both badly and foolishly – badly because foolishly,
Birmingham would say – when they allowed themselves to get so far out
of kilter with the will of the Australian people.

John Birmingham nevertheless does not overplay his hand. He does not
necessarily give any determining significance to Australia's actions in 1975

nor does he countenance the idea of any Indonesian threat to Australia in any conceivable short-term future. This essay is not about the current tumult in Indonesia but John Birmingham believes that the collapse of Suharto's New Order regime left the same power groups ravening through this country which is (beyond Java) effectively constituted by its colonies. Part of John Birmingham's line is that Australia's acquiescence with the Indonesian takeover of East Timor was always unrealistic and likely to endanger relations in the long term more than resistance would have.

Not the least virtue of *Appeasing Jakarta* is the way it counterpoints the realities of a liberal democracy with those of an authoritarian/post-authoritarian regime. John Birmingham does so with a directness and an ethical firmness that is a million miles from all talk of cultural relativism, on the one hand, or region-oriented opportunism on the other.

Appeasing Jakarta is the story of a tragedy and the story of a mistake in judgement, the one compounding and complicating the other. It is not an essay which will please the savants who like to suck up to Asia but it is a polemical essay that happens to coincide with one of the dominant streams in contemporary Australian opinion. It is written in a style that is racy and contemporary, it shows a mastery of that ancient and popular form, the story, and it is consonant in its conceptual clarity with the counter-tradition in Australian foreign affairs thinking, the one that predicted the bloody and terrible result and the advisability (from any point of view) of facing the world with clean hands.

Peter Craven

APPEASING JAKARTA

Australia's Complicity in the East Timor Tragedy

John Birmingham

I did not intend to write this essay. Originally I had something very different in mind, a high-toned review of the prospects for our relationship with that sprawling, problematic neighbour to the north. I had a thesis to run with: the idea that, despite Suharto's downfall and the subsequent elections which swept his party from office, Indonesia was still run – if not ruled – by many of the same interests that thrived under the New Order regime, a network of political, corporate and military players whose welfare and even survival depended on smothering genuine reform. That premise remains an important part of this essay, but it slipped from the centre of my focus as I began to study East Timor, the broken axis around which the relationship turned, no matter how much foreign ministers in both countries might have wished otherwise.

East Timor was the prism through which we viewed Indonesia for a quarter of a century. Earlier instances of contention – Sukarno's

Confrontation and the awful bloodletting of Suharto's ascension to the presidency – supplied uneasy background vision, supplemented by occasional reports of violence and repression in other parts of the archipelago. But it was East Timor which abided, in part because it rubbed at our conscience. Abandonment, betrayal, ineptitude and moral cowardice were all facets of the Australian response to an ill-considered and ultimately ruinous Indonesian adventure, which was less a matter of strategic urgency for Jakarta than a blind run at the main chance by a handful of the regime's power players. You cannot understand the deeply problematic nature of the Canberra–Jakarta link without understanding the history of the East Timor conflict. Many of the pathologies afflicting the relationship today were gestated in the management of that crisis and its long, bitter aftermath.

According to the doctrine of ministerial responsibility, the systemic failure of Australian policy is sheeted home to elected figures, but guilt lies deeper, within the machinery of government itself. While prominent individuals such as Whitlam, Fraser, Keating and Evans all have reason to examine their conscience, the agency which advised, guided and ultimately misled them all was the Department of Foreign Affairs (now Foreign Affairs and Trade). It is arguable that in pursuing what it thought to be a hard-headed assessment of Australia's best strategic interests, the Department in fact undermined those interests by creating a totally unsustainable paradigm for a relationship between a liberal democracy and a para-corporate military dictatorship. Because of the high costs of the democracies' policy towards Adolf Hitler in the 1930s, the word appeasement carries quite terrible connotations today. But it is just a word. A useful one, in fact, for describing a pattern of responses over time. William Maley quotes Donald Watt's modern definition of 'purchasing peace for one's own interests by sacrificing the interests of others'. There is probably no clearer summation of Australian policy towards Indonesia and Timor than those few words.

If it had worked, there might be an utilitarian argument that it was justifiable. But a quarter of a century has shown that there are unbearable costs to appeasing a regime like Suharto's New Order. The long-simmering domestic resentment of Australia's position on Timor evidenced a fundamental flaw in the approach of successive governments. They did not have the support of the Australian people for their policy, only an initial lack of interest in the subject. When the events of September 1999 forced the issue into the forefront of Australian public discourse, the total disconnection between public policy and public sentiment was exposed and a good deal of political energy had to be spent damping down bitterness and fury on both sides of the Arafura Sea. Jakarta's resentment, its sense of betrayal, was entirely understandable, because it rightly considered Australia a friend who had turned on it. Australian anger, in one sense at least, was *entirely unjustified*, because the actions of the Indonesian armed forces and their militia proxies in Timor were simply an extension of a long-established strategy within the former Portuguese colony; a strategy opposed in only the weakest rhetorical sense by Australia, and effectively endorsed by our actions over the decades.

Appeasement of Jakarta did not work because the problem of East Timor was permanent and insoluble. It was assumed before the invasion in 1975 that the East Timorese would accept incorporation. When they resisted, involving Jakarta in a long and brutal counter-insurgency campaign, genuine power realists should have foreseen the ultimately futile and self-destructive endgame which would play itself out there. And some did. But other more significant Australian policy makers, many of whom prided themselves on the 'hard-headed realism' of their analysis and approach, deluded themselves. They chose to ignore dissonant information and analysis from within their own bureaucracy, preferring instead the consolations of wishful thinking. Foremost among their number are Gough Whitlam and Richard Woolcott.

This is not to say that Australia could necessarily have stopped the invasion. Indonesia's takeover had the imprimatur of the United States. It is a moot point whether earlier diplomatic and political action might have headed off the disaster. Suharto himself was not attracted to the conquest and had to be led to it by a coterie of self-seeking palace confidants. Had Australia's official position, which was sincerely sought out and respected by Jakarta, not been based on profound ignorance and the uninformed personal preferences of Prime Minister Whitlam, it is possible that with a major diplomatic effort in 1974 we could have altered the course of Indonesian behaviour. Voices within Canberra were certainly raised to that effect.

Unfortunately, a systemic failure of analysis marked the earliest Australian engagement with this issue, and with the foundation laid it continued to warp Australian policy in the years to follow. It still does. East Timor has gained its freedom, but the wider relationship with Indonesia has been severely damaged and attempts to reconstitute it on the basis of a failed paradigm can only lead to further disappointment. This paradigm – that Australia's strategic interests are served by a partnership with Jakarta *no matter what sort of regime holds power there* – has woven a spell over generations of Australian policy players, both bureaucratic and political. It was never an unchallenged view. But those who held it managed to convince themselves and others that they were the realists and their opponents the dreamers. The reality was exactly the opposite.

By the second half of the 1990s, Indonesia could best be characterised as a crumbling dictatorship, formerly useful as a geopolitical chess piece in the game against communism. With the collapse of the Soviet Bloc, its comfortable position had been eroded, often by its own clumsiness, as in the 1991 massacre at Santa Cruz in East Timor. Three decades of enormously corrupt economic practice had created and exacerbated internal contradictions and fractures along class, ethnic, religious, regional and institutional lines. Such contradictions now see the republic struggling to hold together after the twin blows of the Asian economic meltdown and the disastrous miscalculations of the TNI (*Tentara Nasional Indonesia* or Indonesian Armed Forces) in East Timor. Indonesia's armed forces were never an unfettered power. The New Order was not a pure military dictatorship, more a heavily militarised corporate state. But the TNI, and especially the Army, were a central pillar of the regime. The system rested on their willingness and ability to employ overwhelming violence in pursuit of political ends. The free election that put Wahid in power did not remove the pathologies of the old system; rather it simply introduced new forces and actors contending for control of the state. With no history of managing such chaotic energies which are the lot of democracy, with a shattered economy and beset by the centrifugal forces of micronationalism unleashed by Suharto's downfall, there is no guarantee that Indonesia as we know it will survive the next decade.

Right now, the institution with the best chance of maintaining the unity of the republic is the military, disgraced and sometimes divided against itself. It appears to have learned nothing from East Timor, where its barbarism created the separatist feeling it was trying to suppress. A time may come very soon when Australia will have to face the prospect of dealing with yet another repressive, military-backed regime in Jakarta. If we are not to walk the trail of tears yet again, the story of Timor can provide a rough map of the pitfalls to be avoided. For all the talk of hard-headed diplomats weighing a moral choice against a pragmatic course in 1975, the major question was not moral at all. It was simply: Is this course of action sustainable? It is not really a matter of hindsight to say no. Many advisors predicted the future with telling and ultimately tragic accuracy all those years ago, as this essay will describe. The failure of our foreign policy elite was not ethical, but intellectual. It only became a moral issue when the deficiencies of Australian policy were exposed but ignored for the easier course of appeasement.

There is a marvellous and appropriate comment by George Orwell. Reflecting on W.H. Auden's contemplation of 'necessary murders' in the Spanish Civil War, Orwell wrote that such amorality was only really possible, 'if you are the kind of person who is always somewhere else when the trigger is pulled'. This was the basis of both Australia's moral failure in East Timor and its wider relationship with the New Order regime.

We turned away because the truth was too awful to bear. There were times when I found the research of this essay an unpleasant task. Perhaps because I am a new father, the first-hand accounts of atrocities committed by Indonesian forces against women and children were occasionally impossible to read. They made me nauseous and dizzy. I wondered how policy officers in Canberra were able to read them and live with themselves. The answer, very plainly, was that they convinced themselves of the correctness of their own fantasy, that a reasonably benign Indonesian dictatorship would eventually develop out of soft authoritarianism into a friendly, non-threatening political and economic partner. Evidence to the contrary was nothing but egregious nonsense peddled by anti-Indonesian radicals. It was a policy of wilful blindness, made possible only because we were always somewhere else when the trigger was pulled.

Because of this I have included a fairly long, narrative opening, where the results of self-delusion in both Canberra and Jakarta can be measured in blood, not rhetoric or theory. It is always advisable when politicians of any stripe begin to speak of geopolitics in reassuring generalities to remember that somebody, somewhere is trying to outrun a bullet.

THE DOGS OF LOS PALOS

The Battalion's nickname was strictly and bitterly ironic. 'The Brave Ones'. A fighting unit with a proud history of child murder, rape, plunder and riot. You could tell when Battalion 745 had passed through because of their signature legacy of shallow graves, burnt buildings and drinking wells crammed with the mutilated remains of the dead peasants they were pledged to protect. In September 1999, they were quartered at the eastern end of Timor, at a barracks complex just north of Los Palos, a forlorn sort of place which had never really recovered from the fighting of 1975.

The town, a market centre, sat on a wide plain, a plateau really, the remnant of a huge primordial lagoon which had been pushed up out of the sea with the rest of the island millions of years ago. The ground rose slowly to hills in the south and lay within the confluence of two climatic systems, arid and baking to the north, wetter and somewhat milder to the south. Primal forest survived in these parts, around the base of the mountains where *Falintil*, the armed wing of resistance to Indonesian rule, had retreated before the advancing invaders in '76. Mostly, though, the land was given over to grazing and rice paddies, one of the few areas of Timor not dominated by the soaring, broken-backed cordillera running down its spine. Within Los Palos, low-rise, prefabricated steel buildings threw back the sun's glare as fiercely as the whitewashed limestone walls of the surviving Portuguese architecture, the best of which could be found in a Catholic college about five kilometres north of the town centre. Los Palos had been abandoned by its inhabitants during the invasion, most of them fleeing to the apparent safety of the nearby mountains, and the Indonesians, taking affront, had sacked the town.

Still, as one traveller wrote later, it wasn't so much that Los Palos had been savaged in the war. More that it had been depersonalised, like a settlement at the edge of a volcano's footprint, where the 'habit of living for the moment is engrained'. The people lived here, thought the writer Norman Lewis, not by choice but by an accident of fate, among temporary structures of corrugated iron, and they somehow kept going with a minimum of security and hope. The area had always been a centre of resistance to the invasion. A lot of young boys from Java, Madura and Bali had died around here, and the Indonesian armed forces had taken more than a generous measure of revenge on their behalf. When Lewis journeyed through the district shortly after the travel ban on East Timor was lifted, he found an empty land known locally as the 'dead earth', because those who had filled it were gone. Driving along the coast road, it was possible to see traces of disappeared villages, outlined by strange geometrical beds of wild flowers or phallus-shaped gourds which had grown up within the boundaries of their ruins. Human activity, wrote Lewis, had come to an end.

Battalion 745, the Brave Ones, were tasked by Jakarta with making sure things stayed quiet. They were a territorial outfit, a bunch of second-raters, with a good percentage of their numbers made up by local men. Their training, equipment and operational doctrine were all inferior to the main force units of *Kostrad*, the army's strategic reserve, and *Kopassus*, the fearsome and much-hated special forces. They were not quite as bad as the militia, the military equivalent of those scabrous, stringy-legged wild dogs that haunt the streets of so many towns throughout the archipelago. But 745 were not what you'd call a disciplined or even a remotely formidable military force. Unless you happened to be an unarmed Timorese *paean*. In that case, as Ambrosio Alves discovered on Thursday, 9 September, an encounter with the Brave Ones could be just about the worst thing in the world.

The ninth was a busy day. Nearly a fortnight had passed since the referendum on East Timor's independence, and Jakarta's vengeance, the razing of the new nation, was well advanced. World attention, so distracted in 1975, had hardened against the Habibie government's mishandling of the ballot, but Jakarta seemed to be playing it out, buying as much time as the TNI (the Indonesian Armed Forces) and its militia surrogates needed to finish their work. On that particular day, Indonesian Foreign Minister Ali Alatas called for 'more time' to allow Indonesia to restore order. APEC foreign ministers meeting in Auckland had just demanded that Indonesia stop the killing, but Alatas and his ambassador in Canberra complained that a 48-hour deadline 'was unreasonable'. A fair-enough assessment, given that the 23 000 heavily armed troops and paramilitary police on duty in the province had so far proved themselves entirely incapable of stemming the violence. On the same day, the Australian government, facing a karmic payback on two and a half decades of weasel words and collaboration, announced it was doubling the size of its contribution to any peacekeeping force. The Governor of the 27th Province, Abilio Soares, who had deployed all the resources of state at his command in the effort to secure a vote against independence, said that Indonesia might not ratify the result anyway. TNI chief, General Wiranto, insisted that East Timor had become calmer after martial law, a claim dismissed by the Secretary General of the United Nations and met with weary contempt by the rest of world. The United Kingdom and New Zealand demonstrated their faith in the General's word by dispatching warships to the island; the United States Congress prepared a bill cutting off military aid as UNAMET's (United Nations Assistance Mission East Timor) compound in Dili came under heavy machine-gun fire. The few remaining staff were refusing to leave, saying they feared that one and a half thousand East Timorese who had taken shelter within their walls would be butchered as soon they left. As New York delayed their departure, Jose Ramos-Horta said the United Nations would be leaving them to almost certain death.

The world's attention had pulled in tight on that compound. That was partly a practical matter. There was little else it could see. The UN's regional staff and the hundreds of monitors from human rights groups such as Amnesty and the Carter Centre were going or gone, many of them hustled out of the province at gunpoint by the military. The position of hundreds of journalists, both Indonesian and international, who had covered the ballot and its aftermath, was increasingly untenable as they became the target of vicious harassment.

Matt Frei, from the BBC, described running towards the UN compound as a Timorese man nearby was 'hunted down like an animal'. A colleague of Frei's filmed the attack while hiding in a shack opposite the compound gates. 'It took only 30 seconds to hack the man to pieces,' said Frei. 'The attack was so ferocious that bits of him were literally flying off. The sound reminded me of a butchers' shop – the thud of cleaved meat, I'll never forget it.'

Keith Richburg, from the *Washington Post*, was struck by the resemblance of the Indonesian-sponsored militia to those he had struck in Africa during the Rwandan genocide. He took the blunt edge of a machete in the back from a militiaman while covering an attack near the UN headquarters that reminded him of similar close encounters in Mogadishu. It would all come back to him, he wrote, 'in my room at Dili's seaside Turismo Hotel, barricading the door against intruders, pulling the mattress to the floor to avoid stray bullets, positioning a tree branch near the bed to use as a last defence in case they made it through my flimsy fortification'. He'd left his bullet-proof vest in Nairobi, never believing he'd need it again, 'at least not in Indonesia, not for what was supposed to be an assignment covering economically booming Southeast Asia, in the last year of the century'.

There was one crucial difference, however. The danger in Africa had been random and spasmodic, a wrong place and wrong time deal. But Richburg and the other members of the press corps felt themselves specifically targeted by the military in East Timor, 'to close off the world's eyes and ears, so they could do their dirty work unimpeded'. In Mogadishu, he said, the media could cut a deal with the devil, hiring the militia to protect them as they went about their work. But the same primitive shakedown racket did not seem to operate in Dili. After the machete attack, Richburg and a few colleagues did pay local police, the *Brimob*, to guard the Turismo Hotel where they had holed up. The journalists even ponied up for the cops' meals and drink tab, putting it all on their hotel bill in the hope it might buy a little protection should a posse of goons from the *Aitarak* (or 'Thorn') militia decide to come over the walls. 'But by the third day,' he said, 'one of our protectors confided a secret to *Washington Post* special correspondent Atika Shubert, who speaks Indonesian: If the militia came, he told her late one night, he wouldn't shoot them to save us. He agreed with them, he told her: "They are doing good things for the country."' Richburg decided it was time to leave Dili.

The fact was, a good number of *Aitarak* members were really TNI territorials and *Kopassus*, moonlighting as half-crazed savages who'd run amok after the vote. Various observer groups compiled dozens of statements from East Timorese who recognised members of the Indonesian military in the natty black tee-shirts of Eurico Guterres' nominally private army. The destruction of Dili was so thoroughly well organised and the intimidation and occasionally violent harassment of the observers so finely calibrated that the Indonesian government's obdurate, po-faced denials of state involvement were almost magnificent in their perversity. By the ninth of September however, they had achieved their aim. What the world knew of the crisis in East Timor was confined to a few hundred square metres of downtown Dili, comprising the UNAMET compound and the stories of those trapped inside. Conversely, of course, there was a blowback effect for the TNI. The shadowplay of the militia's vengeance, with the military as puppet master, had drawn the world's attention. Indonesia was getting its fifteen minutes of fame, but for all the wrong reasons. The tactics that had worked so well in earlier conflicts and covert operations, such as the original invasion of the Portuguese colony or the annexation of West Irian, proved less fruitful this time. In '75, Western governments connived at the ruse for geopolitical advantage. Non-aligned Indonesia was valued as an anti-communist foil and allowed or even encouraged in its misadventures. By 1999, a decade after the fall of the Berlin Wall and right after the implosion of the Asian economic miracle, the situation had changed.

The army officers behind the violence miscalculated the effect of their campaign. By forcing the last westerners and such a sorry collection of terrified refugees into the confines of the UN headquarters, they set up a story that the international press, and in particular the American media, was bound to exploit. The fact that the few journalists who remained to report the story got to play both participant and observer, so that they could represent themselves as crucial players in an unfolding tragedy, speaks of a certain lack of forethought on the part of those planning the destruction of East Timor. Indeed, the inability of the Indonesian elite to comprehend the tectonic shifts in both their own polity and the wider world was of critical importance to what happened in 1999, just as it was to the fall of Suharto and as it will be in the next ten years, when their republic either recovers or disintegrates. As Paul Keating stated, around this time Indonesia stopped being a country in US eyes and became an issue. The madness of September '99 simply reinforced Indonesia's new status, as if the violence was an allegory for the disintegration of the whole country.

On the ninth, however, all that mattered was the compound. Throughout the night, the air above was constantly rent by automatic gunfire, with tracers zipping past into the hills behind, making escape impossible. Thousands of people sheltered in a school next door, all fearing an attack which came with militia charging the campus, while TNI troops and Brimob, the paramilitary police, fired on the compound. The panic induced was so great that many parents simply threw their children onto and over the barbed wire which sat atop the wall guarding the UN buildings, hoping to get them away from the marauders. A 26-year-old woman described the assault for Amnesty International after she had been evacuated to Darwin:

> They came in with swords which they were swinging at people, but they did not hit anyone ... The people inside the compound were panicking and some were so scared that they jumped over the fence which had barbed wire on top. Some parents were so terrified for

the safety of their children that they just hurled their babies and young children over the fence. Many of them were cut on the wire or hurt when they fell on the other side. I could see that the army were playing a very direct role in this attack. They were shooting in the air trying to frighten and panic the people and looting all our possessions.

Vision of the attack was beamed out on satellite links, a squalling, claustrophobic catherine-wheel of images. Screaming women and children, wild-eyed men, UN staff and even other journalists - yelling, gesturing wildly for blankets or cardboard or coats, for anything to lay over the wire, all of them flinching and ducking instinctively at the roar of automatic weaponry outside. Only rumours, terrible and perhaps archetypal, relayed any sense of what was happening beyond the immediate range of the cameras. The Guardian's John Aglionby said he'd been told by villagers of men being marched to the waterfront then gunned down and bayoneted, an echo of atrocities from the invasion in '75. Others spoke of bodies, headless and limbless, stacked to the rafters of police stations. Perhaps it was true, but probably not.

The urgency of those horror stories, the way they sparked and jumped so easily from the lips of a terrified refugee and onto the front pages of metro dailies all over the globe, testified to the moral bankruptcy of the Indonesian regime. Their credit was gone, and it says a lot about the attachment psychosis of the New Order regime that it still couldn't help but play out the game. The essence of politics is conflict, but in stable societies this is ritualised and channelled into non-destructive forms. There are limits to action. The New Order, however, which came to power via the enormously bloodthirsty coup and counter coup of 1965–6, seems never to have internalised this lesson, that political development proceeds from anarchy to order – not just to organised terror. At the heart of its extreme reaction to any form of challenge there must have been a corrosive doubt in its own legitimacy. For a regime apparently so certain of its command prerogative, it invested hugely in repressing the merest hints of defiance throughout the archipelago. Freedom was evil, dissent was subversion and its own citizens could not be trusted. That deeply ingrained pattern of political psychosis was allowed a full flowering in East Timor – and so, while the siege of the UN compound in Dili served variously as metaphor and melodrama, and as a channel for the world's frustrated rage, in the dark beyond CNN's failing, constricted field of vision the blood-dimmed tide was loosed. The Catholic Church announced that six nuns in Baucau and a priest in Suai had been slain by militia. The first intimations of a genocidal evil began to seep out of West Timor. And Ambrosio Alves encountered the Brave Ones.

Little is known of Ambrosio's last hours. He was grabbed up in the village of Asalaino by soldiers from Battalion 745 and members of the Team Alpha militia. He was beaten to death and found two months later, in a shallow grave with another, unknown victim. The significance of his passing lies in the fact that he is the first known victim of 745's withdrawal from the province. We know a lot about the passage of the Brave Ones through East Timor because one of their last victims was Sander Thoenes, a Dutch journalist. He had the bad luck to strike a couple of battalion outriders, either territorial or Team Alpha, the same crew who bailed up British reporter John Swain on the second day of INTERFET's (International Force East Timor) lodgement. Swain had hired a taxi with an American photographer Chip Hires and was crawling through the hills outside Dili when 745's convoy enveloped them. Motorcycle riders began hammering at the vehicle, pulling on the handles. One of them turned his rifle on the driver Sanjo Ramos, smashing him in the head with such force that he lost an eye. Swain later said that as Battalion commander Major Yacob Sarosa pulled up, he yelled at the journalists. 'These people are East Timorese too. They are very angry, very angry with [the] UN and you Westerners. You must understand.' The Brave Ones then 'arrested' Swain's interpreter, Anacleto Bendito da Silva, forcing him into a truck at gunpoint. The westerners never saw him again, but a Battalion sergeant, Hermenegildo dos Santos, a *Falintil* informer who later returned to East

Timor, revealed that he had been murdered during the battalion's stopover in Dili.

The Brave Ones were really taking care of business that night. An hour later they're thought to have ambushed Thoenes, the Jakarta correspondent for the *Financial Times*. A local motorcycle chauffeur testified that he gave the Dutchman a lift to the suburb of Becora, where three uniformed soldiers opened up on them with automatic weapons. A single round took Thoenes in the back, ripping through his heart and lungs, causing death within minutes. He was mutilated post-mortem. A nearby TNI post did not intervene in the shooting, or offer the journalist medical aid, nor bother to contact INTERFET.

Between the murders of Thoenes and Ambrosio Alves back in Los Palos, the Brave Ones racked up nearly two dozen civilian kills, some bodies left burning in ditches by the side of dirt roads, some dumped in rice paddies, others in shallow graves or simply in fields where they had been shot in the back while trying to flee. Quite a few dropped down village wells – a disposal technique with a bonus pay-off, the poisoning of scarce water supplies during the island's severe dry season. They made a mistake killing Thoenes, though. One of his freelance employers, the *Christian Science Monitor*, was so appalled that they dispatched another reporter, Cameron Barr, to chase down the story of Battalion 745, which seemed to have marked its route out of East Timor with a trail of corpses and ruin. As he traced their withdrawal, along the coast road and through the dead earth, Barr heard that the Brave Ones had wiped out six people as they swept through the town of Baucau. A young man in Fuiloro, near Los Palos, explained how 745 had snatched up and murdered his brother. Investigators confirmed they were sure the battalion was responsible for Thoenes' death. And in Los Palos he found Sergeant dos Santos, who gave Australian police officers detailed information about his former outfit's war crimes. Barr's reconstruction of the Brave Ones' last days shot holes in the TNI cover story that the unholy disorganised bloodswarm which blew through the eastern half of the island was chaotic, objectless and unplanned. It was, as everyone could see – and as many had warned for months before the referendum – a state-sponsored program, part vengeance and deterrence, but also encompassing barbarism for its own sake. The only question was, which state? The formally recognised government of Indonesia, headed by President Habibie and represented abroad by Ali Alatas? Or another state? A ghost nation existing within the formal structures of the republic, a revenant of Suharto's New Order regime. For that vast, conflicted network of military and corporate combines, well-connected robber barons, state apparatchiks and First Family business concerns did not pass away with the untimely departure of their Emperor. As former Indonesian minister Lakesmana Sukardi put it, 'The pathologies of the previous regime remain in the system.'

This should not come as a surprise. The stripping of formal state power from Suharto and the *Golkar* party was a sea change in the affairs of Indonesia. Given the harsh treatment doled out to opponents as a matter of course during the Suharto era, the eruption of democracy protests in the late 1990s was a testimony to the strength of the pressures building beneath the surface of the republic's polity. But while the removal of the New Order's supreme leader did clear a path into the open for a myriad of challengers, the machinery that maintained him in the presidential palace was not so easily swept aside. Exceedingly powerful economic and political interests were exposed and threatened by the lurch towards democracy. For the New Order was not simply a coercive dictatorship. It also co-opted potential competitors, such as military officers or religious and political leaders, rewarding their allegiance with lucrative positions in the corporate state. Individual beneficiaries of that system might find themselves persecuted as the monolith began to crumble, but the system itself – massive, tenacious and inherently corrupt – was more durable. Speaking in Sydney earlier this year at a seminar organised by the Australia–Asia Institute, the Australian-based Indonesian academic Dr. George J. Aditjondro described the current Indonesian political system as New Order Mark 2, and asked what sort of democratic revolution it was that left the corrupt apparatus of a regime in place. It was this surviving structure which stood behind the carnage in East Timor, mostly because the Indonesian army, which formed one of three pillars of the New Order was, as Bob Lowry put it, still trapped by the formulas of the past. The ham-fisted thuggery of their surrogates' campaign for autonomy, and the savagery of their reaction to defeat, should have come as no surprise. The entire history of the province was leading towards such an eruption, and the brutality of outfits like the Brave Ones was less a matter of uncontrolled rage than finely nuanced policy.

Amnesty International, which devoted extensive resources to covering the pre- and post-ballot period in East Timor, described a 'well-organised plan to remove local residents from one area even before the ballot result was announced'. The smooth meshing of militia and Indonesian government forces gave the lie to Jakarta's denials of any such formal liaison. The day after the vote, in the Aileu District, Police Mobile Brigade personnel drove into four villages 'and began firing into the air'. Amnesty's report continues:

> Militiamen then arrived, ordering people to leave and burning houses down. They gathered people together and forced the people to state whether or not they had voted for independence. Those who had were told that they would have to stay in East Timor and that they would 'die'. In the town of Aileu itself, an observer reported that local TNI officials ordered people to leave their homes, register their names and state which way they had voted in the ballot. They were then told to gather their belongings and move towards the police headquarters in Aileu. According to the observer, one group of people claimed they had been told they would be going to the towns of Atambua or Kupang in West Timor; if they refused to go they would be considered to have voted for independence and would die.

It is inconceivable, given the magnitude and the logistic demands of the scorched earth operation in East Timor, that army chief General

Wiranto was unaware of its existence. The broad outline of the strategy was exposed time and again by foreign journalists and aid workers with direct access to the territory in the months before the ballot.

Operation *Wiradharma*, as it was known to senior *Kopassus* officers, 'would have required at least his [Wiranto's] condonement', according to the United Nation's special investigator, former Australian diplomat James Dunn. Dunn's investigations found that the spasm of 'so-called militia violence' that culminated in massive deportations and destruction in September '99 was not a spontaneous outburst by those who favoured integration, but rather the outcome of a plan by TNI generals, executed for the most part by officers of elite *Kopassus* units. His report found that the Indonesian military sponsored the establishment of the militia, providing training, arms, money and even drugs on occasion.

While Dunn has often been maligned by Suharto apologists as a die-hard member of Australia's East Timor lobby – a charge which did nothing to stop the UN appointing him to such a sensitive position – his report to the UN merely restated the conclusions of Indonesia's own National Human Rights Commission. The Commission reported in January 2000 that there were strong links between the TNI, various arms of the Indonesian police (POLRI and *Brimob*), the provincial government and the militias. The violence was 'the result of a systematic campaign' based on 'extensive planning'. The militias were 'under the direct co-ordination of the TNI', not just one or two rogue, lowly placed officers. Their mobilisation 'was in line with various policies of the military leadership' and 'was accomplished through political terror. Murder, kidnappings and forced displacement were committed by members of the TNI, POLRI, government bureaucracy and the militias':

> After the popular consultation, violence increased drastically throughout East Timor, including murders, kidnappings, rape, property destruction, theft of homes and property, the burning and destruction of military installations, offices and civilian residences, with the goal of forced deportation. Members of the TNI, POLRI

and the militias were the key figures responsible for this campaign which involved the creation of conditions, choice of acts committed, scheduling and planning of the forced deportation. This campaign was initiated to convince the international community that the results of the popular consultation should be doubted and that the people of East Timor would rather choose to live safely in West Timor ...

Of course, that was a choice denied the two dozen unlucky souls who chanced across Battalion 745 on their own journey to the west. The day after Ambrosio Alves fetched up in a hole, two brothers, Florentino and Florencio Branco, were strongarmed out of their village, Home Baru. Their bodies are believed to have been dropped into a well inside the Battalion compound to rest with a few of their neighbours. When Cameron Barr pulled through on the trail of his colleague's killers, he found the well surrounded by tall cornstalks and partially covered over with rusted corrugated iron. It was possible, with the sun in just the right position, to make out the tangle of rotting limbs and torsos at the bottom.

Three days later, another two members of the extended Branco clan joined Florentino and Florencio. On the night of the 12th, Martinho Branco had fled into the rice paddies with his family and their friends, the Belos. 745 tracked them down and fired over their heads, threatening to kill everyone if they made the troops wade through the paddy sludge to lay hands on them. Barr writes:

> The families reluctantly stood up and walked toward the waiting soldiers. Belo and Branco were immediately arrested. Without explanation the 745 soldiers also grabbed each man's eldest child, two teenage boys uninvolved in politics. Juliao de Assis Belo's wife, Filomena de Jesus Freitas, was devastated to see her son in the hands of the soldiers. 'If you want to kill someone, take me, not him,' she pleaded. They ignored her and marched the men and boys along a dirt road that divides two large rice fields. Ms. Freitas and Branco's wife, Maria do Ceu, watched their husbands and sons walk out of sight. Gunshots were heard a few minutes later. The women prayed.

At mid-afternoon Freitas found the courage to go to the Battalion 745 compound to ask after the men and boys. She was told that they had not been arrested. The next day the people in the neighbourhood began to search. At dawn on Sept. 15, they found Belo, Branco, and Branco's son Marcelio in an area about five minutes' walk from where the families had hidden in the fields. The corpses were partially burned, but Freitas recognised her husband's face and trousers. Her son, Elder, was nearby, at the bottom of a well.

The Battalion was occupied for the next few days breaking down their HQ and transporting the bulk of their personnel to Lautem, a small beach settlement by the Wetar Strait, from where they would be shipped back to Java. Those troops remaining in Los Palos ransacked their barracks and burned about three-quarters of the town, including the UN buildings, the market, and the power, water and communications facilities. Their work done, they saddled up a convoy consisting of dozens of army trucks, some stolen civilian vehicles and a few dozen motorcycles – the latter driven by Team Alpha members. Sergeant dos Santos told Barr that the convoy was not filled with overwrought men bent on revenge. The soldiers were happy to leave and indeed seemed delighted with their orders to carry out a scorched earth retreat. As Battalion CO Major Yacob Sarosa stood by, a lieutenant told dos Santos, 'If you find anything on the way, just shoot it.' According to the NCO, Sarosa had previously warned his men that if Jakarta's preferred option went down in the ballot, 'they would have to destroy everything.'

The 21st was the Brave Ones' last full day in East Timor and they held nothing back. It was also a day on which they brushed up close against their own destruction and all but touched off a war between Indonesia and Australia. Their first victims were Abreu and Egas da Costa, murdered just a few minutes after the convoy had left their own barracks ablaze at Laga. Their deaths were witnessed by Zelia Maria Barbosa Pinto, who hid in an irrigation ditch as she heard the convoy approaching. The da Costa brothers, doubling on a motorbike, weren't as lucky. Their own engine noise masked the approach of the trucks until it was too late and the battalion outriders were on top of them. Somebody in the convoy yelled out that they were terrorists, and as Abreu backed away from the motorcycle and screamed at his brother, 'We're going to die,' the soldiers opened up on them.

Someone shot Abreu's leg out from under him as he ran. He fell, staggered up and made it a few more feet before a round slapped into the back of his skull and pitched him into the paddy water. His brother didn't get that far; he was shot in the stomach before he could run more than ten feet. Zelia Pinto watched a soldier walk over and bayonet him.

The da Costas had been about a hundred yards from the turn-off to their home in the village of Buruma. But it's a moot point whether they'd have lived if they'd made their run just a few minutes earlier. 745 moved inexorably through Buruma and the sister village of Caibada that morning. Lucinda Da Silva took a shotgun blast in the chest. Elisita da Silva was machine-gunned while cowering behind a bush with her baby daughter, Cesarina. The toddler's grandmother witnessed the shooting, which killed Elisita and shattered Cesarina's right thigh. A few miles down the road, a couple of soldiers straggling behind the convoy killed Victor Belo, who was returning to his home thinking the danger had passed. Carlos da Costa Ribeiro, a former teacher who had stayed hidden in his house, was hunted down and shot in the head.

Later in the day a couple of Timorese youths, who remain unidentified, were arrested, beaten and taken to Manatutu. They were never seen again. The village itself was annihilated, with 98 per cent of the buildings razed to the ground. When the UN came through a few days later, not a living soul could be found in Manatutu and the surrounding countryside appeared to have been emptied of life.

745 and Team Alpha drove through the old Portuguese quarter of Baucau, the second city of East Timor and a major staging point for TNI operations throughout the centre and eastern reaches of the island. From there they took the coast road west for Dili, where they bundled up the

journalists Swain and Hires, before killing their colleague Sander Thoenes. As the convoy moved along the main Becora road, with gutted, burned-out houses slipping by on both sides, soldiers in the back of the trucks whooped it up, firing into the air. A local who was caught out in the open, Manuel Andreas, was shot in the back as he tried to escape down a ruined side street. The convoy halted for a few hours at the TNI barracks in Dili, where they refuelled, ate dinner and murdered John Swain's interpreter. Before they drove out later that evening on the last leg of their retreat, a local military commander asked them to refrain from further bloodshed. Within half an hour they had driven into a potentially catastrophic showdown with the second cavalry regiment of the Australian Army.

The Australian modified light armoured vehicle, the ASLAV to its friends, is really not that light. Or friendly. It weighs in at about thirteen tons, depending on its configuration. 2 Cav, the Second Cavalry Regiment of the Australian Army, runs up to half a dozen variants based on three different hull types. The ASLAV 25, an eight-wheeled, three-man reconnaissance vehicle, carries an M242 25 mm Bushmaster cannon, a chain gun which can discretely place a single high-explosive incendiary cartridge into the heart of a problem, day or night, from up to 2000 metres away. Alternately, should you prove reluctant to come around to the Cav's way of thinking, the Bushmaster could hose you down at a rate of 200 rounds per minute. The ASLAV 25 can also mount two machine-guns in its turret, which is fully stabilised and equipped with a thermal imaging day/night gun sight. Its sister vehicle, the ASLAV PC, which is designed to carry seven troops into harm's way, comes with a 12.7 mm machine-gun and a day/night gun sight at the Crew Commander's station. Standing next to an ASLAV, your average machete-wielding villain is immediately dwarfed by its blunt mass and, more subtly, by the promise of mayhem contained within its brutish frame. As the Australian Army's Third Brigade secretly worked up a concept of operations for lodgement in East Timor (a week before President Habibie invited them in), 2 Cav's thirteen-ton armoured vehicles were among the first units chosen.

The ASLAV's offensive capabilities and the training and commitment of the men who drove them were the reasons why armed peacekeepers were never going to be welcome in East Timor in the pre-ballot period. General Cosgrove made it abundantly clear at the start of INTERFET's mission that trying to intimidate his soldiers would be a very different matter to lording it over unarmed civilians. With a neutral, heavily armed force in place, the TNI's scorched earth policy would have been prohibitively expensive, or even impossible to carry through in the face of opposition from the likes of the Second Cavalry Regiment. The antipathy and reserve of the Indonesian forces which prevailed in Dili when INTERFET arrived was partly an expression of that. The TNI had many more troops in place, but behind the comparatively small number of INTERFET personnel stood the threat of intervention by the armed forces of those states that had contributed them, including (though not limited to) Australia's traditional allies, the United States and Great Britain. The appearance of that foreign armour on Dili's ruined streets signalled to all sides in the East Timor conflict that things had changed; specifically, the immunity to armed sanction enjoyed by pro-Jakarta forces had ended. This transitional phase was the most dangerous moment of the crisis, the point at which miscalculation by INTERFET or foolhardiness by militia or TNI units could easily flash into a wider, international conflict. Into this situation rode the Brave Ones.

On the night of 21 September, the second day of INTERFET's mission, half a dozen ASLAVs, disbursed in two groups, were squatting astride the main east-west road through Dili. While the TNI's senior officer in East Timor, Major General Kiki Syahnakri, had proved entirely co-operative and had indeed rendered invaluable assistance to INTERFET during the taut period immediately before and after the arrival of Australian combat forces, Dili was still infested with hundreds of militia bandits and ill-disciplined Indonesian troops. At all hours of the day and night they tore through the devastated city in trucks and cars, screaming abuse and levelling their weapons at the Australians. Under the rules of engagement they could have been shot at any time for making such threatening gestures, but the Australian troops restrained themselves despite the heat and stress and physical demands of carrying full combat loads. That stress should not be underestimated. Foot patrols ran all day and night. Sleep was snatched in short bursts among rubble and burning refuse. Bob Breene, in one of the first serious military accounts of the INTERFET mission, described the environment as an assault on the senses. 'Smoke, stench and dust filled nostrils and stung eyes. Buildings were on fire or smouldering black shells.' Rubbish, dead dogs and human filth lay everywhere, piled up into mounds wherever large numbers of East Timorese had sheltered in the last hours, such as down at the port. Very few civilians remained in the town proper and nobody walked anywhere. Everyone ran. Night-time was even weirder. 'Bizarre and dangerous', according to Breene, a city of the dead under a smoky red glow, with long convoys of trucks crammed with soldiers and loot rolling through the streets while spasmodic gunfire and explosions could still be heard in the distance.

The first Australians ashore, an advance group of about 1500 paratroopers, special forces, assault pioneers, cavalry and airborne infantry, worked in a hyper-stressed, uncertain atmosphere. Indonesia still had tens of thousands of armed men on the ground, and despite Syahnakri's genuine desire to avoid any conflict, everyone was aware that these were the same troops General Wiranto had supposedly had so much trouble controlling over the past month. Ramping up the tension, the Australians, most of them very young men, were at last close enough to reach out and touch the material consequence of the TNI's failure. Bodies rotted in drinking wells, drainage ditches and ruined buildings. Some, writes Breene, had been burned to destroy evidence, leaving behind nothing more than ashes and bone.

Some bodies bore signs of torture and all had been mutilated. In some cases, hands and heads had been cut off in a crude and brutal attempt to hide the victim's identity. The body of a young woman, her hands bound and throat cut, abandoned in a toilet area awash with her blood, was a shocking discovery for the diggers who found her. For many young soldiers these were the first bodies they had seen. Soldiers who had to recover and place remains in body bags, or re-bury bodies for health reasons, recalled that they would never forget the smell and how it lingered on their clothing long after they had finished their gruesome duties.

In some buildings there were signs of multiple murders, the dark brown of dried blood accentuated by white tiled floors. At several sites floors were covered in blood and gore; bits and pieces of people. There were thick sprays of blood and brain tissue along walls at a height suggesting that victims had been forced to kneel before being shot through the head. Limbs, chunks of flesh and entrails were scattered about in other buildings amongst pools of blood suggesting frenzied attacks with knives and machetes. The diggers followed blood trails of victims who had been hacked, and then fled, bleeding profusely before succumbing to further blows; dying before their bodies were dragged away. There were machetes and clubs covered in gore, abandoned after being used to butcher victims. Bloody drag marks suggested that scores of bodies had been dragged away for disposal.

In contrast to the 23 000 TNI and *Brimob* troops, who had been strangely ineffective in the face of this slaughter, INTERFET's comparatively small number of personnel began locking down the city immediately. The ASLAV roadblock was part of a campaign to quickly establish their dominance. The armoured carriers were parked in a herring-bone arrangement at two sites to snare single truckloads of militia and others who still haunted the city in the first few days. The soldiers manning the road block had orders to stop anybody who was armed but not in uniform. They had no idea that Battalion 745 was coming through the night towards them.

Around ten o'clock in the evening, the Brave Ones' motorcycles, riding point on what had grown into a 60-truck convoy, ran up hard against the ASLAV checkpoint. After looting and killing their way across the island from Los Palos, 745 and their Team Alpha cohorts were emotionally unprepared for any resistance. They'd been ordered to chill out back at the Dili barracks, but as the convoy growled and squeaked to a halt in the dark, angry militiamen and soldiers began to shout and wave at the Australians, demanding they move aside. The Brave One's vanguard presented as a sort of B-movie vision of some pirate biker gang from Hell, a rat bastard outfit in black tee-shirts, camouflage pants, long hair and bandanas, with axes in their eyes and guns at the ready. The Australians – assault pioneers, a couple of rifle platoons and six pairs of snipers – were all kitted out with body armour and night vision equipment, giving them a distinctly threatening, insectile, otherworldly appearance beneath their kevlar helmets. Unbeknownst to the territorials and militia, who were blind in the dark, their every move was being observed in the cool green glow of low-light amplification systems.

The Australian ranking officers, a pair of lieutenants, one of whom spoke Bahasa, informed the motorcycle escort of his orders to detain anyone they came across armed and not in uniform. The riders revved their bikes as their spokesman blustered and demanded passage through the blockade. The voices grew loud and more agitated as it became obvious that 745 might not be allowed through immediately. As more Australian soldiers quietly deployed to support their leader, Indonesians and Timorese dropped from the backs of trucks, unshipping their weapons, crying out, demanding to know the cause of the delay. Some of the hard chargers of Team Alpha and 745 began to shoulder their rifles, unaware they could be seen in the dark.

Under the UN-sanctioned rules of engagement, they were now dead men. But the Australians, outnumbered many times over, did not open up on them. They did not respond in any obvious way. No orders were given, but each man slowly raised his Austeyr F 88 from the hip. Guns on the ASLAVS tracked around smoothly, settling on the trucks full of Indonesian soldiers. Photon streams poured out of laser designators, painting bright dots – visible only through the diggers' night vision goggles – on the foreheads and chests of those men fated to die first.

As INTERFET commander Major General Peter Cosgrove said later, it is no exaggeration to say that the future of Australia's relationship with Indonesia hung in the balance for the next few minutes. Besides 745's military personnel, those trucks also carried the family members of some departing soldiers. Mixed in with their heavily armed, undisciplined escorts, many would have died in a fire fight. So tenuous was the situation in Dili, and so poisonous was the relationship between the two countries at that moment, that everything then turned on the actions of the young lieutenants and the men standing behind them.

The Howard Government was well aware of the potential for such an incident to spin out of control and had warned the Australian electorate to prepare itself for heavy casualties. Instancing the sort of scenarios that could unfold, a Current Issues Brief prepared by the Parliamentary Library's Foreign Affairs, Defence and Trade Group on 21 September contemplated a range of outcomes in the territory, including high-level armed conflict between the Australian Defence Force (ADF) and the TNI.

> If such a worst case scenario were to eventuate the consequences could initially include booby traps, land mines, snipers, maritime mines in or around the harbour, low-level skirmishes, ambush, mortars, and attacks launched from shoulder launched surface-to-air missiles. INTERFET could face terrorist attack, for example, a truck bomb driven into an INTERFET compound or hand grenades thrown into a town market. If the TNI directly confronted the ADF and the situation escalated, the ADF would probably seek close air support which would include attacks on the TNI from helicopter gunships. The TNI in turn could seek air support and Indonesian F-16s could confront ADF F-18s over the skies of the territory.

The paper went on to dismiss such a possibility as remote, mostly because the Indonesian armed forces were significantly outclassed by the ADF in such capabilities. But the spectre of disaster was ever present with heavily armed, keyed-up members of the two forces intertwined in such a volatile setting. It needed only one misfortune to escalate, such as the unanticipated 'capture' of Battalion 745 in the ASLAV's militia snare, and all of Cosgrove's and Syahnakri's efforts at a smooth handover would fall through. Escalation was avoided in this case only when the Australian command decided to allow the convoy through.

Cosgrove has used the example of this roadblock more than once to illustrate the importance of training, discipline and modern equipment. He saw it, quite rightly, as a small moment of vindication. But it was also a failure, a nexus point at which the full weight of twenty-four years of accumulated strategic folly, moral poverty, infamy, lies, naïveté and self-delusion suddenly dropped onto the shoulders of a handful of young soldiers.

It had long been an unspoken tenet of Australian strategic guidance that while this country probably would not lose a war with Indonesia, it certainly could not afford such a conflict. The relative capabilities of each nation's military forces actually favour Australia, a point to be explored later. But Australian policy makers have long understood that as a small, white outpost of the former British Empire, Australia's place among its neighbours cannot be taken for granted. Colonialism left a bitter taste in the mouths of many nationalist leaders in the region, and Australia's long commitment to the White Australia Policy still rankles – even though it is the most egregious form of hypocrisy for some regional states to claim the moral high ground on matters of racial tolerance.

In spite of excellent ties with powers such as Japan and Korea, Australian interests can still be damaged by the hostility of individual states. For instance, Malaysian Prime Minister Mahathir's implacable opposition to Australian initiatives such as APEC has seen our diplomats barred from a number of important regional forums and trading groups. In the 1990s, our close relationship with Indonesia, the first among equals in ASEAN, counterbalanced such antagonism. Australian commitment to regional institutions and operations such as the peace plan in

Cambodia demonstrated a willingness to work with and for the region, and lent credence to Prime Minister Keating's oft-stated conviction that we should seek our security within Asia, not from Asia. For a few months in late 1999, that admirable objective was threatened by developments in East Timor. For a few minutes on the night of 21 September, it was in mortal peril. The gulf between Australia and Indonesia was already yawning when President Habibie bowed to world pressure to allow a peace-keeping force into the disputed territory. How much greater would the chasm now be if somebody's trigger finger had twitched that night?

So Cosgrove was right to praise the cool professionalism of his men, which certainly avoided a crisis and quite possibly a catastrophe. But they should never have been placed in such a position to begin with. That is not to say that they shouldn't have been sent to East Timor, rather that their presence and the grossly magnified consequences of any miscalculation on their part evidenced the collapse of the dysfunctional paradigm embraced by successive Australian governments for managing the relationship with our northern neighbour.

Australian policy, which once encompassed the likelihood of armed conflict with Indonesia as a leading principle, has long sought to avoid such a disaster. This is entirely commendable. Without a commitment to large-scale immigration, Australia's relative strategic standing can only decline over the next century. Consequently, to adopt an adversarial posture towards Indonesia – or whichever state succeeds it, should the republic fragment in the next decade – would constitute the most inept and negligent of stratagems. Consider just some of the relevant geopolitical factors – the increasingly violent atomisation of Melanesia and Polynesia, the institutional decay of Papua New Guinea, the inevitable implosion of North Korea, nuclear competition on the subcontinent, the manifold uncertainties of communist China's future, and the decreasing importance of New Zealand as an economic and military partner. There are precious few reasons for optimism. Even putting aside geopolitical threats, the unavoidable marginalisation of Australia's tiny economy will erode what little leverage it can apply to international affairs at the moment. To be forced to manage all of these challenges while maintaining a bilateral cold war against Indonesia or its successor states would be beyond our capacities.

Herein lies the motivation of a generation of Australian diplomats, soldiers and politicians who struggled, vainly as it turned out, to put aside elemental national differences in the attempt to forge a mature and practical concord between two mismatched nation states. No dishonour attaches to them for making the attempt, but the model adopted, which can be characterised by its wilful blindness towards permanent flaws in Suharto's New Order regime, was of questionable value. Indeed, many questioned our approach to East Timor when it arose as an issue. But it is only now, with that newborn nation in ruins and ties to Jakarta ripped asunder, that the costs of our misjudgment can be quantified. Of course, the prime responsibility for the carnage in East Timor, not just in '99, but over the preceding two and a half decades, lay with the Suharto government and its schizoidal offspring, the interim administration of Habibie. But Australian governments of all political hues bear responsibility for their actions, which gave succour to tyranny in the belief that diplomatic pragmatism demanded nothing less. That the outcome of this failure was not a heavy reckoning in Australian blood and treasure is a testament to the skill and courage of the ADF – and, it must be emphasised, to the efforts of many Indonesians who were determined to avoid the siren song of xenophobic nationalism.

Despite the longstanding and blatant frustration of political elites in both Canberra and Jakarta that the relationship was held hostage to the fate of a small island nation both would rather have forgotten, the fact remains that a hostage it was, and even now remains. East Timor was the prism through which everything else was viewed. It both distorted and defined the relationship between the two countries, and before turning to the future we are obliged to try and understand this past.

There are two men on whom the burden of consequence falls most heavily. Gough Whitlam, Australia's Prime Minister at the time of Indonesia's initial moves against the colony. And Richard Woolcott, a First Assistant Secretary in the South Asia Division of the Department of Foreign Affairs from 1973–4, a Deputy Secretary from 1974–5, Ambassador to Jakarta from March 1975 and later the Secretary of the Department itself. The Whitlam Government keenly appreciated Indonesia's strategic significance to Australia. Among its many foreign policy initiatives was a program of constructive engagement to minimise differences between the two countries and, it was hoped, to build on the many areas of common interest. Whitlam's somewhat imperial style of diplomacy should be viewed in the context of his reformative mission. He wanted to improve Australia's foreign relations as much as he wanted to reform her domestic arrangements. In Woolcott he found a willing partner in the Foreign Affairs bureaucracy, a man whose character encompassed a singular fusion of idealistic patriotism and hard-headed expedience.

Woolcott has refused to accept a heavy share of the responsibility for Australian policy towards Indonesia and its 27th Province. He points out, quite correctly, that as a bureaucrat he merely advised his ministers and implemented their policies. But this significantly undervalues his own contribution. It is disingenuous in the extreme to suggest that as a central player who promoted his own counsel with perseverance and great energy, he was little more than a factotum. The documentary evidence portrays a man with a sweeping, ultimately flawed, vision of the road best travelled to secure Australia's interests. He was a patriot but a strictly utilitarian one. For Woolcott, the measure of an argument was not to be found in its ethical consequences, but in its effect on immediate Australian concerns.

Between them, Woolcott and Whitlam laid the foundation for a tragedy. They did not do so with malice. They believed then, and probably still do, that the actions they took in the 1970s were the best for Australia – and even for East Timor, all things being equal. They were not unpatriotic or self-abasing in their dealings with Jakarta. They attempted to balance a dreadful burden of competing claims and pressures. They acted out of the highest motives, with the future of all Australians as their primary concern. But in doing so, they led us into shame and towards peril. With the restrictions clamped on East Timor after 1975, however, it would be many years before the nature of the evil at work on that island was truly revealed at the Santa Cruz cemetery on 12 November, 1991. By then Australia had become so mired in the original sin of accommodating the takeover that only by the most wrenching and painful effort could we tear free. It heightens our disgrace that we did not.

It was just a little massacre, was Santa Cruz. Nineteen dead. Maybe fifty. Or perhaps, two or three hundred. Such a trifling thing, really, in comparison with the bloodletting at Matebian and Kraras, at Liquica in May of '76, at Suai, Maubara, Basartete. And of course at Lamaknan. ABRI really extended themselves at Lamaknan. Two thousand dead in one day. The torn-up bodies of women and children coiled promiscuously with the remains of the men who had been unable to protect them. So a dozen, maybe a couple of dozen, or even 271 killed, 278 wounded, 103 hospitalised and 270 'disappeared' ... well, it was a *comparatively* trivial massacre, was Santa Cruz.

There were a few crucial differences, however. For a start, the army was sloppy. They killed a bunch of journalists in 1975. But let them escape in '91. The eyewitness accounts of the American reporters Allan Nairn and Amy Goodman, supported by video shot and smuggled out by Yorkshire Television's Max Stahl, were the sort of spin doctor's nightmare that Jakarta and its western backers had never really had to face before. With East Timor a closed province through the 1970s and '80s, the army had been pretty much free to do as it pleased and it pleased them to kill off maybe a third of the population while trying to convince them of the advantages of Indonesian citizenship. This genocidal policy was what western leaders sometimes euphemistically described as being 'in the best interests of the East Timorese people'.

In 1991, however, the cover story fell apart. Nairn and Goodman had travelled to the territory hoping to cover the visit of a UN and Portuguese parliamentary delegation. The army had made it plain in hundreds of meetings in villages across the island that they would not tolerate any-thing other than a clean report card. According to Nobel prize winner Bishop Belo, ABRI (*Angkatan Bersenjata Republik Indonesia* or Indonesian Armed Forces) as the TNI was then known, colourfully threatened to hunt down the families of anyone who tried to demonstrate or speak out and exter-minate them 'to the seventh generation'. Many young men, stupidly brave as young men tend to be, defied them, taking refuge in the seaside church of San Antonio de Motael. When the delegation's visit was post-poned, the army stormed the church, killing one of the occupants, Sebastiao Gomes, with a point-blank gut shot.

A number of journalists were still in East Timor over a week later when Gomes' funeral procession made its way through Dili. The UN Special Rapporteur on Torture, Pieter Koojimans, had arrived in Dili the day before, and the Timorese resistance had decided, somewhat recklessly, that his presence would protect them should they turn the funeral into a demonstration. It didn't. As the funeral was winding up, hundreds of Indonesian troops advanced on the mourners and opened fire. ABRI spokesmen later claimed that they had been provoked by the stabbing of one of their own, but that line was demolished by Stahl's video, along with Nairn and Goodman's independent testimony which was given added currency by their prominent injuries.

In sworn testimony to the US Senate Committee on Foreign Relations on 17 February, 1992, Nairn described an unprovoked assault on a mass of defenceless civilians including young men and women, children in Catholic school uniforms and old people in traditional dress. There were between three and five thousand of them, a defiant, unheard-of spectacle.

Older men constrained the exuberance of youth, shouting 'Disciplina! Disciplina!' at any boys threatening to become too excited. After the church service, as people milled about talking among themselves, an ABRI troop truck sealed off the exit to the graveyard. The background noise level dropped as conversation died and the tramp of boots crunched towards the cemetery:

> Then, looking to our right we saw, coming down the road, a long, slowly marching column of uniformed troops. They were dressed in dark brown, moving in disciplined formation, and they held M-16s before them as they marched. As the column kept advancing, seemingly without end, people gasped and began to shuffle back. I went with Amy Goodman of WBAI/Pacifica radio and stood on the corner between the soldiers and the Timorese. We thought that if the Indonesian forces saw that foreigners were there, they would hold back and not attack the crowd.
>
> But as we stood there, watching as the soldiers marched into our face, the inconceivable began to happen. The soldiers rounded the corner, never breaking stride, raised their rifles, and fired in unison into the crowd. Timorese were back-pedalling, gasping, trying to flee, but in seconds they were cut down by the hail of fire. People fell, stunned and shivering, bleeding in the road, and the Indonesian soldiers kept on shooting. I saw the soldiers aiming and shooting people in the back, leaping bodies to hunt down those who were still standing. They executed schoolgirls, young men, old Timorese; the street was wet with blood, and the bodies were everywhere.

At this point both Nairn and Goodman were also targeted. Troops ripped away their equipment and grabbed fistfuls of the female reporter's hair, punching her face and kicking her in the stomach. As Nairn attempted to protect her with his own body, he was smashed with the butts of the soldiers' M-16s, fracturing his skull. He was covered in blood, his entire body in spasm as the troops yelled 'Politik! Politik!' and 'Australian! Australian!' Mindful of 1975, Goodman shouted 'No, American!' and threw her passport at them. It seemed to work, perhaps, Nairn thought later, because their attackers' M-16s were made in the USA. They were allowed to flee, with the sound of gunfire still hammering the air and the East Timorese being slaughtered around them. Goodman later described the scene for her radio listeners:

> They moved on and they killed the Timorese who were moving, not able to run away but not yet dead. They dragged an old Timorese man next to us and they beat him into the sewage ditch behind us. Every time he could get up he would put his hand in a prayer sign and they take their rifle butts and smash them into his face. He would still climb up out of the sewer and try again to get out and they would beat him down. Every time we picked up our heads to look it seemed that more infuriated the Indonesian soldiers so we kept our eyes to the ground. The whole road had become a killing field ...

They hopped a jeep and truck and headed for the hospital with dozens of Timorese hanging from the sides, the cabin, the spare tyre. All of them desperate to clear the area.

> We drove like that, as a human mass, to the hospital. In the hospital we saw the lucky Timorese. The Timorese who were wounded but not yet dead ... the Timorese who had their arms shot off ... whose backs were blown open but they were there. The first little boy to go down ... the first person as the Indonesian soldiers had opened fire right behind us... was about 6 or 7 and he had his hands up in the V sign as they just shot him until he exploded.

It was, Nairn testified, a deliberate mass murder. There was no provocation, no stones were thrown, the crowd was quiet and shrinking back as the shooting began. 'This was not', he insisted 'an ambiguous situation that somehow spiralled out of control. The soldiers simply marched up in a disciplined, controlled way and began to fire massively on the crowd.'

You could trace the Indonesian government's dawning realisation that something had changed by the shifting rhetoric and body count after

Santa Cruz. Professor Antonio Barbedo de Magalhaes, of Oporto University, Portugal, quotes the Commander-in-Chief of ABRI, General Try Sutrisno, speaking at the National Defence Institute within twenty-four hours of the massacre. 'They are people who must be crushed,' he said. 'This scum must be eliminated ... come what may, they cannot ignore ABRI ... ABRI is determined to eliminate anyone who creates disturbances.'

The unqualified support or even just the slightly embarrassed silence and foot shuffling which such a statement might have attracted earlier was missing this time. The US Senate called on President Bush to support an immediate resolution in General Assembly, 'instructing the United Nations Commission on Human Rights to appoint a Special Rapporteur for East Timor'. Fifty-two of the 100 senators signed a letter to Bush asking him to give the troubled province much greater attention and to 'intervene more actively'. European countries cut off aid. The ACTU organised boycotts and supported the establishment of an East Timorese 'embassy' just outside Indonesia's own embassy in Australia, much to the fury of Foreign Minister Gareth Evans. Suharto was forced to backtrack, establishing an inquiry. Its findings of nineteen killed were ridiculed around the world and a further inquiry had to be mocked up, this time admitting to fifty deaths.

The survival and testimony of the westerners was the crucial axis around which reaction finally turned to the Indonesian military's record of barbarism. But the motive power for that change of direction was not simply the impact or novelty of Stahl's images or the American reporters' words. The decision that changed the course of Indonesian history was not taken in Dili, Jakarta or Washington. Rather, the impetus came when Mikhail Gorbachev pronounced a death sentence on the old Soviet Union by embracing the twin policies of *glasnost* and *perestroika*. As the Iron Curtain was figuratively torn down and the Berlin Wall literally demolished, the frozen structures of a bipolar political world began to thaw and creak into movement as well. A string of tinpot third-world dictators soon discovered that there was little or no gratitude in Western capitals for the sterling support they had offered freedom's cause by sterilising any trace of socialist contagion within their own domains. The New Order regime had long enjoyed a protected place within that system, and as news of the Santa Cruz massacre leaked out Jakarta was wrongfooted by the outraged global response.

Nothing changes overnight, of course. The US had deeply invested in Suharto's rule, and her vast national security bureaucracy was never going to react to change as nimbly as, say, US media organisations (which had largely ignored the story of both Timor's invasion and Indonesia's own holocaust in 1965). While publicly condemning the Santa Cruz killings, the Bush Administration urged Jakarta to spin up a reactive public relations campaign. A month after the massacre, at a secret meeting in Surabaya between US and Indonesian military officials, the Americans commiserated with their hosts and reassured the worried men that although Indonesia might have been under considerable pressure, 'we do not believe that friends should abandon friends in times of adversity.' Meeting U.S. Ambassador John Monjo on Christmas Eve that year, one of Suharto's principal advisors thanked the diplomat for his government's support. That support was both moral and material, with both the State Department and the Pentagon angling to double military aid to Indonesia through IMET (International Military Education and Training) funds, arguing that this would expose Indonesian military officers to 'democratic ideas and humanitarian standards'.

In spite of all this, however, the US had soon cut off Jakarta's access to American military aid. The impetus came from Congress, which began to take heat for the relationship. An ad hoc network of Churches, activists, students and exiled Timorese lit off a grassroots campaign to change the course of US policy, inundating the House Foreign Operations Subcommittee with more representations on East Timor than members of Congress received on any other issue at that time. Both Republican and Democrat members began to move in response to the massacre and its aftermath. Christians were outraged by the desecration of the Church in East Timor. Democrats came under pressure from civil rights campaigners and union organisers. Companies such as Nike might have appreciated the New Order's robust approach to labour relations, with the occasional headless labour leader floating downstream to ensure that sneakers selling for a hundred dollars in Los Angeles could still be made for five in Jakarta. But American unionists did not take kindly to it. And American members of Congress with American unionists in their districts certainly didn't.

Of course, the crucial point here is the awakening of American opinion. Not Australian. That had always been the case, both after Santa Cruz and during the original crisis in 1974–5. Australian public opinion and the Australian media were of one mind in 1975 and 1991. But the Australian government was acting to a different script, hoping to muddle through the initial blaze of outrage. For all of Australia's sense of shame and self-doubt over its role in '75, however, only one power could have vetoed the annexation of Portugal's former colony: the United States of America. And it chose not to. President Ford and Secretary of State Kissinger privately encouraged the invasion. The US Ambassador to the United Nations, Daniel Patrick Moynihan, crowed about his role in blocking enforcement of UN demands that Indonesia withdraw from East Timor. Noted human rights advocate Jimmy Carter sold lethal Marine Corps counterinsurgency equipment to the Indonesian military when it became bogged down in its own private Vietnam. And a long, distinguished list of American statesmen from Vice President Walter Mondale through to William Jefferson Clinton actively supported both the regime and its policies in the 27th Province, all the while parroting the prodigiously witless excuse that this was in the best interests of the East Timorese.

While much has been made of a meeting in September 1974 in which Australian Prime Minister Gough Whitlam is supposed to have given Suharto the impression Australia would not oppose incorporation, a more important conference took place just twenty-four hours before the main thrust of ABRI's attack went in. President Ford and Henry Kissinger spoke with Suharto on their way out of Indonesia after a state visit. Kissinger has denied that Timor was even discussed. However, during a function in New York on 11 July, 1995 to publicise his book *Diplomacy*, he was ambushed by Allan Nairn who was still smarting over being touched up by the Indonesian military at Santa Cruz.

When Kissinger replied to a question about the invasion by saying 'Timor was never discussed with us ...' Nairn jumped to his feet. He had ferreted out an official State Department transcript of the conversation with Suharto which made it clear the invasion was discussed. More damningly, President Ford himself had told Nairn that together he and Kissinger 'gave US approval for the invasion of East Timor'.

The reporter waved another memo, this time of an 18 December, 1975 meeting held at the State Department that exposed Kissinger 'berating' staffers for recording a finding that the invasion violated international law as well as a treaty with the US, because American weapons were used offensively. Nairn carried on for some time before Kissinger finally rode over him, saying, 'Look, I think we all got the point now.' When the reporter asked whether Dr. Kissinger might support convening a war crimes tribunal on the subject of East Timor which could examine his own conduct, the flabbergasted Machiavellian could only bluster in reply. 'I mean, uh, really, this sort of comment is one of the reasons why the conduct of foreign policy is becoming nearly impossible ...'

Thumping the podium, the former Secretary counter-attacked. 'Timor was not a significant American policy problem. If Suharto raised it, if Ford said something that sounded encouraging, it was not a significant American foreign policy problem. It seemed to us to be an anti-colonial problem in which the Indonesians were taking over Timor and we had absolutely no reason at that time to pay any huge attention to it.'

The reasons for this official US disinterest in 1975 and during the bestial crusade of subsequent years are in fact well known and accepted by stakeholders on both the left and right. The US, as Kissinger went on to point out, was preoccupied with the fall of its favourite domino, South Vietnam, in April of that year. Suharto's machine had established its anti-communist credentials in 1965 by slaughtering somewhere between five hundred thousand and one million communists along with fellow travellers, political rivals, illiterate peasants and unlucky bystanders. Despite Jakarta's eminent position in the non-aligned movement, Washington valued Indonesia as a strategic counterweight to China. A practical demonstration of the Suharto government's bona fides in this area was the unrestricted movement they allowed American nuclear subs through deep ocean passages within their territorial waters. This enabled the Pentagon to move its nukes between the Pacific and Indian oceans safe from detection by satellite. One such passage ran north of Timor. As long as US foreign policy was shaped by the Cold War, the tiny half-island state was damned. Where then did Australia fit into this?

Despite a strained performance encompassing synthetic outrage and denial, the Whitlam government was nearly as well informed as the Indonesian Cabinet about the upcoming annexation of Portuguese Timor. The documentary history of Australia's reaction to the takeover, released by the Department of Foreign Affairs and Trade (DFAT) in 2000, makes this abundantly clear. (It also resonates with the crisis of 1999, another decisive point at which official Australian knowledge of Indonesian state duplicity and malign intent was ignored as naive hopes won out over long experience).

In 1975, there were members of Suharto's ministry who were undoubtedly less well informed than senior figures in Canberra. Some of this intelligence was gathered clandestinely, through signals intercepts and espionage. A good deal of information was publicly available through the media. But by far the most important source of Australian government knowledge was Indonesian government collaboration. Two men in particular kept the Australian Embassy in the loop: General Benny Murdani, head of the Strategic Intelligence Centre within the Indonesian

Department of Defence and Security and Harry Tjan from the semi-government Centre for Strategic and International Studies (from which emanated much of the actual planning for the takeover).

It is all too easy now to perceive in Jakarta's actions of that time an ill-considered adventurism. With memories of Sukarno's Confrontation and Suharto's bloody crackdown of '65 still fresh, that was a common enough perception shared by both the left and right in Australia in the mid '70s. But in fact Suharto had to be talked into annexing the territory by the Tjan and Murdani faction and was assiduous in seeking out the opinion of all possible stakeholders. As the largest neighbouring country, with the region's most capable military and close ties to the US and European powers, Australia was not ignored. The Whitlam Government had placed a good deal of emphasis on improving and broadening the relationship with Indonesia, and the two heads of government had developed a good rapport. It was a relatively anaemic precursor to the friendship that blossomed much later under Keating, but it was warm, courteous and considerate when measured against the chill of the Sukarno period and the suspicious and occasionally spiteful decade after the invasion. In this climate it shouldn't be surprising that Canberra was kept abreast of developments to the north. What is surprising is the extent of that access.

So closely appraised of Indonesian manoeuvres, both covert and open, was the Australian Department of Foreign Affairs, that occasional spasms of panic would grip them when they realised how thoroughly compromised they were by this intimate knowledge. At times ministers and diplomats were forced into the ludicrous position of maintaining a stone-faced detachment while they publicly accepted Indonesian government denials of operations which both knew full well to exist. As Ambassador Woolcott would write in a cable in late October 1975, 'Although we know it is not true, the formal public position of the Indonesian government is still that there is no Indonesian military intervention in East Timor. If the Minister said or implied in public the Indonesian Government was lying we could invite a hurt and angry reaction.'

In early July of 1974, a full year and half before the invasion, Harry Tjan had told Jan Arriens, the First Secretary at the Australian Embassy in Jakarta, that he intended to submit a paper that week to Suharto recommending Indonesia 'mount a clandestine operation in Portuguese Timor to ensure that the territory would opt for incorporation.' In a letter from the Australian Ambassador of the time, Robert Furlonger, to Foreign Affairs back in Canberra, the diplomat revealed that Tjan had high hopes for Australian support in neutralising adverse reaction among third countries to any takeover and in convincing the UN to formally recognise the new arrangements. Tjan was quite explicit about the tactics the Indonesians would adopt. The discussions with the Australian Embassy had not been initiated by the Indonesians, but they had seized the opportunity, according to Furlonger, 'to try to take us along on a *realpolitik* approach to the problem'. He continued, 'they are speaking surprisingly frankly. We are, in effect being consulted. They clearly expect a response from our side: a failure to do so soon will be taken by them, I fear, as tacit agreement.'

In reply, Graham Feakes, First Assistant Secretary, South Asia Division, warned the Ambassador that, valuable as the contact with Tjan had been, he should in no way be encouraged 'to talk to us along those lines'. Australia simply couldn't afford to be associated with any Indonesian covert action in the colony. He had doubts about whether such an operation could even succeed and wondered whether the kudos which would attach to Tjan and the Centre for Strategic and International Studies might 'distort rational thinking and assessment of the risks'.

The information flow continued, however. Just before the invasion, Feakes wrote a submission to Foreign Minister Don Willesee, specifically addressing the question of the intelligence that was still pouring into the Embassy through Tjan and Murdani. Willesee, who was more sceptical of Indonesian ambitions than his Prime Minister, feared that by supplying the information the Indonesians had put Australia in the position of 'conniving with them in their military intervention'. Feakes thought the fear well-founded, but had altered his position over the intervening year or so. He thought that the flow had been so great for so long that to stop it now would not substantially reduce any charges against the government of conniving with Jakarta. The information was also proving invaluable in gauging Indonesian intentions. And suddenly to freeze out the two men at that point might give the Indonesians reason to think that Canberra wanted to change the nature of the relationship, which was already suffering strain over developments on the island.

If you read through the collection of documents released by DFAT in 2000, one of the clearest impressions they give is a sense of policy slippage, as Canberra found itself increasingly trapped by the sort of dilemmas exercising Willesee and Feakes in October '75. Before September of 1974, Australia did not even have a policy on East Timor, and a good deal of bureaucratic and political effort went into avoiding the creation of one over the next year. On dozens of separate occasions, different players advised against being drawn into the emerging problem, created by a coup in Portugal, that led to the accelerated decolonisation of East Timor.

The sincere desire not to become embroiled in any crisis on the island was immediately undermined by the Indonesians' steady background feed of briefings and intelligence. Nor was it ever likely that the Government would be able to opt out of a role, given the robust nature of Australian democracy which, unlike the Indonesian situation, allowed for the total spectrum of opinion on political matters to be aired, no matter how inconvenient and embarrassing it might be for the government of the day. Finally, as Ambassador Furlonger had written, the Indonesians having informed Australia of their intentions would 'clearly expect a response'.

What they received from Whitlam in his meeting with Suharto at the State Guest House in Yogyakarta in early September of '74, was a curious, two-tracked reply which, being entirely contradictory at its core, was naturally interpreted by Indonesia to suit its own ends. The official Australian record of the meeting has Whitlam telling Suharto that the PM's own views would likely become government policy. It continues:

> The Prime Minister said he felt two things were basic to his thinking on Portuguese Timor. First he believed Portuguese Timor should become part of Indonesia. Second, this should happen in accordance with the properly expressed wishes of the people of Portuguese Timor.

In those two simple and totally irreconcilable statements lay the contradiction that would bedevil and warp Australian foreign policy and contribute to the violent oppression of the East Timorese people for two and a half decades. Although Australian ministers and diplomats repeatedly spoke of the requirement for consultation with the East Timorese, they also repeatedly emphasised that Australia placed primacy on its relationship with Indonesia and thought that the best result would be an Indonesian takeover. Furthermore, by allowing the Suharto regime to believe that the sort of perverse facade which passed for a popular consultation in West Papua would also suffice in East Timor, a situation arose whereby Jakarta assumed it had Australia's support not just for their move against the former colony but for whatever tactics they chose to employ. Australia had, after all, been kept well informed by Tjan and Murdani.

When Major General Ali Murtopo, the head of OPSUS, the special operations outfit that engineered the covert action against East Timor (as it had in West Irian), met with Australia's Ambassador to Portugal, Frank Cooper, in mid-October 1974, he told Cooper that Whitlam's visit to Jakarta and his support for incorporation had helped the Indonesians 'crystallise their own thinking and they were now firmly convinced of the wisdom of this course'. According to the Javanese General, they had been undecided about Timor until that meeting with Whitlam. Perhaps, then, Whitlam's comment that 'for the domestic audience in Australia, incorporation into Indonesia *should appear* [my italics] to be a natural process arising from the wishes of the people', was, under the circumstances, a little ill-advised. When dealing with the same group who had killed up to a million of their own people in coming to power, and who had routinely used bribes, threats and physical violence to make the incorporation of West Irian *appear* to be a natural process arising from the wishes of the people, you really want to choose your words carefully.

The disordered policy response continued even as paratroops began to drop on Dili, sparking reports of mass killings, summary executions and widespread atrocities. Instantly the game shifted to reaction, to the stance the government would now have to take. It's strange, but with hindsight the roles of the actors in this part of the drama have become obscured rather than clarified. With Australian domestic politics still dominated by the supply crisis of the Whitlam Government and the subsequent election campaign, bureaucrats tended to command centre-stage more than might otherwise have been the case. Chief among them of course was Richard Woolcott, the Ambassador in Jakarta from March '75, who became something of an archfiend in the mythology of the Australian left and among the coalition of interest groups routinely belittled as 'the East Timor lobby' by commentators such as the *Australian*'s Greg Sheridan.

In fact, although Woolcott can stand duty as a figurehead for those advocating acceptance of the annexation, it should be stressed that none of the actors involved fit perfectly into those categories assigned them over two decades of emotive conflict. The story of Timor was a tragedy with elements of farce, horror and villainy on all sides. It is not, however, amenable to simple conspiratorial explanations – such as the oft-repeated accusation that Australia was primarily motivated by a desire to cut Portugal out of negotiations for the Timor Gap oilfields. Such complicated, fearful and uncertain episodes are pregnant with the potential for myth-making. Political myths, as the late Murray Edelman famously explained, are unquestioned beliefs held in common by a large group of people which give complex and bewildering events a particular meaning.

Political events, on the other hand, generate heat, light, sound, fury and a surfeit of anxiety – especially in the treacherous realm of affairs between states when they relate directly to such intimate and powerful concerns as national survival. Myths give order and meaning to this threatening chaos. They replace 'gnawing uncertainty and rootlessness with a vivid account of who are friends, who are enemies, and what course of action must be pursued to protect the self and significant others'.

Woolcott features prominently in the political mythology of East Timor, mostly as a duplicitous, antipodean facsimile of Henry Kissinger. His own references to 'Kissingerian realism' did him no favours in this respect. Nor did his prominence in the aftermath of the Balibo killings. The murders of those five Australian-based journalists fuelled a lasting antipathy within the Australian media towards the Suharto regime and more generally towards the Indonesian state. Indeed, it is arguable that had those men simply been captured and 'detained for their own safety' while their equipment was destroyed, the course of Australian–Indonesian relations might have run much more smoothly. But the presumed murders, and a shambolic Indonesian cover-up in which the complicity of Australian officials was automatically assumed, set an entire generation of journalists against the New Order regime and any Australian attempt to deal with it from any basis other than a vaguely hostile reserve.

As the diplomat at the forefront of attempts to ensure a working relationship with Indonesia after the invasion, Woolcott has worn the ignominy of association with the disgraced regime, at least in the thinking of the Australian Left and among supporters of East Timorese independence. But Woolcott's failure – and the failure of the Australian governments that followed his advice – was not, as even he portrayed it, an ethical delinquency. It was first and foremost an analytical failure from which moral consequences then evolved. For all of Woolcott's 'Kissingerian realism', for all of his claims to a hard-headed 'sophistication and maturity' in the formulation of national policy, and for all the years he has defended the line of argument he put to Canberra as the only practical course at that time – he was wrong. Hundreds, maybe thousands of individuals played a role in determining the course of Australian engagement with Indonesia after the Suharto government decided to seize the former Portuguese colony. A few key figures have had the misfortune of being loaded up with the full weight of consequence flowing from that. Driven in part by Woolcott's own insistence on the impossibility of alternative approaches, a perception has grown of a monolithic, undifferentiated opinion prevailing on the subject in Canberra, a sort of diplomatic flying wedge which simply mowed down anyone in its path. Again, it is a seductive image, but misleading.

Hundreds of voices were raised in warning against the dangers of collaboration with Jakarta. It is obvious from the mass of communications generated by Woolcott and available in the published DFAT collection of East Timor documents that even he was alive to some of the risks inherent in the course he advised. He simply judged those risks worth taking in the national interest. Others did not, and here we find a crucial flaw in the power realist argument that Australia had no alternative but to accept the takeover and move on. This opinion – and it was nothing more than that – was based on the assumption that Indonesia would prevail with relative ease and that the invasion and annexation would be accepted without significant opposition within Timor or elsewhere. It was a premise that was by no means universally accepted within the Australian government, and events quickly exposed it as little more than an expedient conceit.

As early as 11 December, 1974, at a policy discussion among the most senior bureaucrats of the Department of Foreign Affairs, the wretched future of Indonesian intervention was being laid out for discussion. Of course, at that point the participants had no idea what would actually happen, but the prescience of some was almost preternatural. Gordon Jockel, then Director of the Joint Intelligence Organisation and Ambassador to Jakarta between March '69 and February '72, warned that Timor could become a 'running sore' for Indonesia. It was a phrase that recurred with depressing regularity and increasing frequency as time passed. Minutes of the discussion record Jockel's warning that:

> The situation was very different from West Irian, many of the inhabitants had military training (1000 in the army, 15 000 formerly in the army and therefore with some military experience, and 3000 in the reserves who received regular training); given the nature of the terrain it would be easy to mount and sustain a liberation movement with outside support. If a liberation movement did in fact develop, it would gradually attract international attention and Portuguese Timor would become more of an international issue ...

Our own military history should also have sounded an alarm. In 1942, three hundred Australian commandos of the 2/2nd Independent Company took to the same mountains that *Falintil* would later haunt. Their guerrilla campaign killed at least one and a half thousand Japanese soldiers for the loss of forty Australian lives. More importantly, the commando's presence drew another 30 000 Japanese to the territory who were then unable to be deployed elsewhere and who proved to be incapable of neutralising the guerrilla threat anyway. The tactics employed by the 2/2nd were almost a blueprint for later *Falintil* operations; with the Japanese response, the slaughter of tens of thousands of Timorese peasants, constituting a macabre anticipation of ABRI's own actions.

Jockel may have had this in mind when he added that, while he had sympathy for the Indonesian position, they risked alienating those not in favour of integration and pushing them into 'some form of extreme action'. And this was a full year before the invasion and the drawn-out saga of oppression and atrocity began.

Michael Cook, First Assistant Secretary, North and West Asia Division, agreed with Jockel. His contribution was most telling. He pointed out that at the first meeting of division heads, 'no one knew much about Portuguese Timor. There seemed to have been a basic assumption that

Portuguese Timor would be like West Irian; the people would accept integration, and from this assumption followed our commitment to an internationally acceptable act of self determination'. [My italics] However, it was now clear, said Cook, that the East Timorese were not malleable, integration was not a winnable goal, and the situation itself was changing as people reacted to the possibility of an Indonesian takeover. Cook now thought 'that in the long run independence would be better than integration'.

Kenneth Rogers, the First Assistant Secretary, Defence Division, took up the issue of the contradiction at the heart of Australia's two-pronged policy. He thought 'too much emphasis was placed on Australia's interests all being best served by its [East Timor's] incorporation into Indonesia', and warned that states often ran into difficulties after incorporating additional territory, depending in large part on the method of incorporation. Rogers thought that in preparing future positions, 'the incompatibility of the two policy objectives should be explained more fully ...'

Outside Foreign Affairs, especially within the Defence Department, others also had their doubts. In a paper on the defence significance of the island, Bill Pritchett, First Assistant Secretary for Defence Planning, wrote in early August 1974 that he thought Australia's best interests were served by supporting an independent East Timor, even though this would place stress on the relationship with Jakarta. He was entirely dismissive of any concerns that it could become a Cuba of the south, as the Indonesians and defenders of Australia's actions have frequently argued. The geopolitical reality was that any government in Dili would have to align itself according to the wishes of its two larger neighbours. In an even more prescient memo, written to his Minister Bill Morrison in December 1975, he demonstrated a grasp of logic that seemed to be entirely lacking in many of his colleagues in DFAT.

While Australia's best interests were served by maintaining good relations with Indonesia, Pritchett wrote, our contradictory policy actually threatened those relations. 'Since the weight of evidence from the outset has been that any act of self-determination would oppose integration, in effect what we have offered Indonesia with the one hand we have sought to deny them with the other.' The lethal flaw in Whitlam's policy contrivance was never more effectively laid bare. Pritchett went on to predict the exact course of events in the colony. *Fretilin* would remain the dominant opponent and Indonesia would only take the island with such force that it could not be hidden from the Australian public, generating strong opposition here. Any hope that Jakarta might resolve the matter quickly and without repercussions 'appears increasingly misplaced'.

Foresight was not restricted to Woolcott's fellow bureaucrats. Whitlam's Cabinet colleagues were in no way as sanguine as he was about the prospects of a fair resolution. Lance Barnard, Deputy Prime Minister and Defence Minister during the Whitlam Government, produced an almost oracular analysis of the evolving crisis in a letter to fellow sceptic, Foreign Minister Willesee in February '75. Outlining what he saw as the consequences of any 'immoderate action' by Indonesia, he predicted such a negative response by such a wide range of Australian domestic opinion that it would severely limit Canberra's chances of maintaining even existing ties. 'Years of effort to induce a sober and responsible approach for the development of a constructive relationship ... could be undone.'

It's arguable that Whitlam should have foreseen this himself when press reports of an Indonesian training run for the invasion produced a gust of outrage and anxiety here. However, rather than projecting this into a wildly rancorous sequel should there be an actual move against Portuguese Timor, Whitlam instead told Suharto directly in April 1975 that, 'he did not like the way in which the Australian people, in the face of the rumours of an invasion of Portuguese Timor, had been shown to be overly nervous and fearful of Indonesia'. It was, he said, an unnecessary and unwarranted reaction to the rumours in the press. When added to his statements that good relations with Indonesia were of 'paramount importance to Australia', that 'he could not help feeling the majority of the people of Portuguese Timor had no sense of politics, and that in time they would come to recognise their ethnic kinship with their Indonesian neighbours,' such words must have further 'crystallised' the Indonesians' thinking.

Barnard, by way of contrast, had no trouble understanding the dangers of ambiguity in Australian posturing and Indonesian thinking. In the course of his long letter to Willesee, two months before Whitlam's April meeting with Suharto in Townsville, he wrote that Jakarta's military plans were based on 'quite unrealistic assessments' of the dangers of a radical *Fretilin* administration in East Timor. He wrote that 'the principal factors stimulating the developments feared by Indonesia are the attitude and behaviour of Indonesia itself.' The other reason Australia found itself in a bind, he thought, was that Jakarta heard only 'so much of what we have said to them as they wanted to hear, namely our acceptance of their interest in the future of Portuguese Timor and of its eventual absorption into the Indonesian state.' He advised, as did Willesee later, that Australia should try to moderate Indonesian fears of an independent East Timor, as well as make it abundantly clear that we opposed the use of military force there. It would have been a major shift from the original two-track policy, but in the end it did not happen. Suharto left his April meeting with Whitlam convinced that the number one priority for Canberra was, as Richard Woolcott argued so often and so successfully, good relations based on an understanding of the difficult Indonesian position.

In July 2000, at a conference organised by the New Zealand Institute of International Affairs to examine the consequences of East Timor's referendum and its aftermath, Woolcott allowed himself 'one self-indulgence' in explaining that he was not an apologist for any other country. He was, as *Time* magazine had described him, 'a wattle-proud patriot', not an 'appeaser of aggression' as some would have it. After somewhat disingenuously reminding the audience that ministers, not officials, make policy, he then mounted a brief and well-practised defence of Australian actions in the 1970s. It was not appeasement, grovelling or apologising to try and 'introduce balance and sensitivity towards large and complex regional countries in the throes of major political, social and economic transitions'. The development of sound relations with those countries – Indonesia, China and India foremost among them – was a fundamentally important national interest. 'This should not involve any compromise with our own values,' he said, 'but it does involve seeking to understand – not necessarily to approve – but at least to understand the policies and motives of these important nations.'

Nobody would take issue with that, or presume for a moment that Woolcott or Whitlam – or later figures such as Fraser, Peacock, Keating or Evans – approved of what happened in East Timor. But it does seem, from the comfortable vantage point of the present, that in 1974–5 others had a deeper understanding of Jakarta's 'policies and motives' and what they would mean for ties with a democracy like Australia. The sorrow and the enigma of this story is why they didn't prevail.

While Woolcott was never a simple appeaser nor a mere cipher for a discredited world view, he seems inexplicably obtuse about the outcomes of Australian policy on Timor and Indonesia, a policy which he helped shape (whatever he might say about the respective roles of ministers and their servants). For someone who told his listeners in New Zealand that foreign policy was more properly concerned with outcomes than aspirations, he seems to have missed the results of twenty-four years of painfully contorted Australian policy around the wreckage of East Timor. Aspirations and outcomes?

I mean, really. What were you thinking, Mr Ambassador?

It was an all-consuming aspiration to remain onside with the Suharto regime which led directly to the ruinous outcomes predicted by so many players, including Pritchett, Barnard, Rogers and Jockel. It was the aspirations of Ali Murtopo, Benny Murdani and a cabal of para-corporate military fixers, palace courtiers and opportunists which led to twenty-four years of genocidal warfare against the people of East Timor. And it was the aspirations of the Timorese people themselves, discounted in the first instance, to live in peace and later simply to survive, which led to what Habibie described as the gravel in Indonesia's shoe. The continuing insistence of policy-makers throughout the 1970s and '80s that incorporation was the best result for everyone recalls historian Barbara Tuchman's withering comment on King Phillip II of Spain, that no experience of the failure of his policy could shake his belief in its essential excellence.

At what point, one wonders, might faith in the excellent notion of Indonesian annexation have been shaken? In the weeks before open invasion, when the Timorese proxies and Indonesian 'volunteers' who swept over the border ran headlong into a *Falintil* blocking force which then inconveniently failed to melt away, bottling up their advance with heavy Indonesian casualties in the western districts? Or perhaps in the opening hours of the air assault on Dili, when reports of extensive massacres of civilians could still get to the outside world? Was faith in our excellent policy tested in the following weeks, as thousands of Indonesian troops died in the mountainous countryside and thousands of Timorese perished in reprisal? Did anybody in the Department of Foreign Affairs have any doubts about the hard-headed realism of accepting the takeover when Jakarta was forced to go cap in hand to the US to beg for specialised counterinsurgency equipment such as the Rockwell Bronco OV 10? The Bronco, which had proved itself in Marine Corps operations against the Viet Cong, was put to sterling use by ABRI delivering payloads of high explosive and napalm onto the sides of mountains and into deep, inaccessible valleys where tens of thousands of Timorese had fled from their advance. Did anybody ask themselves whether the profligate use of these aircraft, which carry up to 3600 pounds of assorted bombs, cannon, missiles, and machine guns on 5 underwing hard points, might betray a certain level of desperation on the part of ABRI? Did it occur to any policy makers who learned of the bizarre and medieval 'Fence of Legs' operation in March–April 1981 that here was a regime it might be best to treat with some caution? After all, what sort of a relationship could we really have with a government that used as human shields 80 000 people it claimed as its own citizens. When intelligence reached Canberra that ABRI had forced this many Timorese to walk in a line from one end of the province to the other, in an attempt to round up the resistance like a bunch of errant scrub turkeys, did it give anyone pause? Did the huge numbers who died from starvation and exhaustion in this hideous absurdity leave so much as a scratch on the 'big picture' at which Canberra was so fond of staring? Could anyone who read George Aditjondro's description of the Fence have any doubt that here was a punitive overlord acting not out of pressing strategic urgency, but simply from base ugliness and a malignant will to power?

> Those fleeing from the advancing Indonesian troops and their East Timorese human shield often had to abandon hundreds of children and babies, who mostly died of starvation because their parents were killed by the Indonesian soldiers, or who were killed by their own parents because they were afraid that they would slow them down, or because their crying would put everyone else's life in danger, or because there was simply no more food to feed them.

Did anyone in authority ask themselves, as hundreds of thousands were herded into concentration camps to deny *Falintil* a base of popular support, whether our excellent policy of hard headed-realism might rebound one day? It is obvious that Jakarta either did not ask or did not care whether it was creating a population so embittered by their experience of Indonesian rule that they could never accept it in their hearts. But one wonders whether any of the experts in Australia who had experience of Vietnam asked themselves the same question and pondered the advisability of becoming Suharto's stalking horse with our *de facto* and then *de jure* recognition of Indonesian rule. Did the Timorese famine of 1979, as severe as those in Biafra and Cambodia, cause even a slight shudder of moral repugnance to run up the spines of those who advocated that recognition?

You may be surprised to learn that the answer is yes. The moral quagmire of formally recognising Indonesian sovereignty was a source of heated debate between various players in Canberra and its embassies.

In May 1977, nearing the end of his assignment to Lisbon, Ambassador Frank Cooper sent a secret AUSTEO ('Australian Eyes Only') cable to Canberra and the missions in Jakarta, Washington and New York, questioning whether any Australian government could ever sell a policy of recognition to the electorate. If the Fraser government decided to recognise what it had previously condemned, he wrote, 'the question many people will ask is not whether we can live with it but whether we can live with ourselves.' Woolcott, who seemed more than a little put out to be thrust into the role of the antipodean Kissinger yet again, shot back that the resolution of the Timor issue was not simply a black and white moral choice and asked what possible national interest was served by withholding *de facto* recognition of what major powers and other regional countries had already acknowledged – that East Timor was now part of Indonesia.

This exchange took place as ABRI's invasion mutated from a violent but conventional conflict in which many of the thousands of civilian deaths could be counted as collateral damage, to an overwhelmingly brutal counter-insurgency campaign directed at an entire renegade population. Debate within the Australian government over the level of casualties in this period betrayed a chronic low-level angst about the wisdom of past policy and the suitability of any future line that Canberra might adopt. In the face of this, the power realist doublethink and amoral sophistry embraced by Foreign Affairs also betrayed the maturing of a dysfunctional mindset that had its origins in the policy settings first articulated in 1974. The repetitive restatement of Whitlam's view that good relations with Jakarta came first, and that East Timor would be better off opting for Indonesian rule by a genuine vote had placed a fracture deep in the centre of Australian strategy which was never resolved. As that contradiction became more painful, the ethical and intellectual contortions required to maintain it eventually demanded a response. The response was denial.

Denial that the death toll could be that high. Denial that the atrocities could be that bad. Denial that a modern state, with which we sought close relations, could pursue so destructive an end by such vile means. Denial that by recognising its sovereignty over the island we were approving of its actions. And denial that we had been besmirched by our failures, by our foolishness, our clumsiness, our cowardice and our gross moral turpitude.

It might seem odd that a highly structured, rational organisation such as the foreign service could fall prey to the sort of delusional states which we think of as individual maladies. But organisations, and in particular exactingly formal hierarchies such as the military or diplomatic corps, are in some ways more vulnerable to capture by their own mythology. They may serve liberal democracies, but they are not themselves either liberal or democratic. They are rigid structures in which power, status and autonomy are accrued by gradual advancement through the ranks. Formally, this advance is based on merit, informally it is dependent on an officer declaring for a set of assumptions, beliefs and norms of behaviour that constitute the culture of an organisation. Except in the most dysfunctional outfits, those assumptions and beliefs will have a solid basis, but from that anything might grow. And if through weakness or folly some crisis has escalated to a point where it threatens the organisation, both theory and history tell us that rigid hierarchies will tend to react, not with realism, but with recourse to some consoling mythology. Intelligence agencies and national security bureaus have an especially long and undistinguished history of refusing to accept information that does not accord with their established beliefs, of suppressing such intelligence or even fabricating data that does fit more agreeably. By smothering dissent within and discounting it from without, by refusing to question first principles and insisting on the primacy of the corporate line no matter what evidence of its inadequacy might surface from time to time, the Department of Foreign Affairs and the successive ministries which followed its advice, all joined hands and stepped through the looking glass into a wonderland where their failure was negated through the expedient device of proclaiming it a success. In this unbecoming process lies the link between the mistakes of two Australian governments – one Labour and one conservative – and two cataclysms which befell the people of East Timor. Herein too lies a warning for any future governments which accept without question the orthodox creed that good relations with Jakarta are of paramount concern, regardless of what sort of regime holds sway there.

By the time the Howard Government was required to actually respond to the mess in East Timor with action rather than rhetoric and duplicity, the framework for dealing with Jakarta was rusted in place. The principles adopted a quarter of a century earlier – a retreat into tunnel vision, the denial of hard truths, a refusal to plan for worst-case scenarios – were all established as standard operating procedure within Australia's foreign service. To genuinely question them would mean undermining the accepted and bipartisan foundations of Australian foreign policy. To overturn them would effectively require the declaration of a bureaucratic holy war on the Department of Foreign Affairs. It is unsurprising, then, that Howard, who seemed so much more comfortable engaging with domestic rather than international politics, was largely content to let DFAT run with their proven game plan. While he doubtless counts securing East Timor's freedom as a highlight of his term in office, the government response appeared to be a catastrophic shambles from the vantage point of a contemporary observer. For this he can blame his Foreign Minister's underlings.

The various misjudgments of the Howard government in the lead-up to the referendum in East Timor are nowhere more savagely dissected than in a paper by William Maley, from the Australian Defence Force Academy's School of Politics. Writing in the *Australian Journal of International Affairs* in the aftermath of the TNI's scorched earth retreat, Maley destroyed any claim Howard might have tried to make to having achieved a positive outcome in East Timor. Running just beneath the surface of Maley's argument was a similar forensic assault on the wisdom of Foreign Affairs' dominant paradigm – what we might call the Woolcott line – while admitting the injustice of loading up one man with responsibility for the accumulated decisions of many actors over so long a period. Even though he does not specifically draw them out, when reading Maley you can't help but be struck by the parallels between the errors of 1975 and 1999.

Some are strikingly obvious. Just as warnings of a military and humanitarian disaster were disregarded in '75, predictions of another catastrophe in '99 were likewise glossed over. Foreign policy specialists might well pay less heed to public sources such as the media or the many independent observer groups that flooded the province in the months before the vote. But what excuse can there be for ignoring their own sources? As Coral Bell from the Strategic and Defence Studies Centre has pointed out, Australia's relevant intelligence agencies – the Office of National Assessments, the Defence Intelligence Organisation, the Australian Secret Intelligence Service and the Defence Signals Directorate – were all warning the government as early as April '99 'that widespread violence was likely, and that the militia in East Timor were really auxiliaries of the official Indonesian army, so that responsibility for their activities was not a matter of "rogue elements", but went right to the top in Jakarta.'

There even seems to have been a reluctance to engage our alliance partners on the issue, lest American pressure for peace-keepers to land before the ballot upset Jakarta. The fatuous suggestion by one unnamed Australian diplomat that inserting peace-keepers would be a disincentive for the opposing sides in East Timor to sort out their differences reveals the depth of official cluelessness and denial in the foreign affairs bureaucracy. As Bell argues, 'the implication that Canberra was initially overly optimistic about both the likely reaction in Jakarta to a vote for independence, and about its own level of influence there, seems to accord with a long-established pattern, characteristic of Australian governments of both parties vis-a-vis Indonesia.' Again, you can only wonder at the capacity for self-delusion of supposed professionals who could watch with equanimity a series of manifestly state-sanctioned atrocities such as the attack by Eurico Guterres' *Aitarak* militia on the home of the pro-independence Carrascalao family. With television beaming the obscene vision of one victim's gaping, lipless abdominal wound into the lounge rooms of mainstream Australia, the famous analytical skills of our highly trained foreign service seem to have been less effective than the common sense of the mass of people. As Maley put it, you did not need to be an Indonesia specialist to anticipate disaster in East Timor. 'Elementary reasoning was enough to establish that the approach being taken by the Australian government was quite extraordinarily dangerous.'

Was nobody listening when the leadership of the TNI-sponsored militia promised civil war at a rally in February? The problem, as Maley says, 'was not a dearth of evidence, but a fear of accepting that it pointed to disaster'. Ian Martin, the head of UNAMET, put it succinctly when he admitted that the violence was widely predicted by those who eventually delivered on their promises, 'but most of us were reluctant to believe they meant what they said.'

Maley lists a number of principal misjudgments by the Australian government in 1999 which are worth repeating because of the eerie sense of *déjà vu* surrounding them. He was speaking only of the referendum period, but the points he makes are equally applicable to the original annexation. It is hard to understand, he asks, why Canberra thought pushing through with the ballot would strengthen the relationship; just as Canberra once thought that endorsing an Indonesian takeover would strengthen ties with the New Order. In both '75 and '99, Australia fundamentally overestimated the weight Indonesia placed on maintaining good relations. It also erred grievously in assuming that Jakarta was acting according to a simplistic 'rational actor' model of behaviour. In both cases, those responsible in Jakarta were driven by deeply felt but essentially irrational motivations – national pride bordering on hubris and a fear of instability infecting the rest of the archipelago. The primary cause of Indonesian instability is not regional resistance to the central government *per se*, but the militarisation of that resistance in response to the TNI's 'exporting' the tactics it refined in East Timor to other flashpoints such as Aceh. In spite of the established preference of the New Order for violent repression as a standard operating procedure, there was no indication that the policies of either government, Whitlam's or Howard's, involved 'any comprehensive weighting by DFAT of potential benefits against potential costs as far as the East Timorese people were concerned'. Maley writes of 1999 that, 'there appears to have been a constant reliance on the most optimistic assumptions and a disinclination to consider less attractive alternatives. Yet any worthwhile realist – let alone a Machiavellian – analysis of the situation clearly pointed to the possibility of disaster.' Again this analysis applies perfectly well to the administration of Howard's ideological nemesis, Gough Whitlam.

The long persistence and cross-party nature of this problematic template raises the question of how much responsibility lies with the elected officials who supposedly made that policy and how much with the professional bureaucrats who supposedly implemented it. Maley identifies four systemic problems within the foreign affairs bureaucracy which had fossilised in place long before John Howard wrote to Habibie supporting the idea of a referendum in East Timor. An obsession with the idea of the 'big picture' was and often still is 'used as a rationale for wishing away uncomfortable realities'. The rigid hierarchy of the Department of Foreign Affairs and Trade severely discourages questioning of certain orthodoxies, or what I would call myths. The Department is still entranced with the mystique of its own communiqués, preferring them to competing sources of information which, naturally, do not always concur with the company line. And finally, there is 'a tendency in DFAT to muddle through and hope for the best, rather than to engage in proper contingency planning'.

Examining the Howard Government's performance in early 1999 in the light of these factors, certain ambiguities resolve themselves. On the one hand, there is evidence of confusion and hopelessness – such as the scorn poured on Portuguese concerns about the TNI's capacity or willingness to provide genuine security and the refusal to countenance placing real pressure on Jakarta to accept peace-keepers before the ballot. On the other hand, Howard presumably authorised certain actions such as the reported 'black' surveillance flights that so upset Jakarta, and possibly even special forces reconnaissance missions as reported in the British press. Howard and his Defence Minister John Moore were quick to claim credit for placing Australia's armed forces at a much higher state of readiness, thereby facilitating the rapid deployment of INTERFET. And indeed credit is due, because this action was completely out of character with the established model for handling volatile situations in which Indonesia is a party principal. It contrasts starkly with the complaints of US State Department official Stanley Roth that Australia's approach was defeatist and raises the possibility of both doctrinal and tactical differences between the bureaucracy and the executive.

That it took destruction on such a massive scale to finally break the hold of a long-established paradigm on Australian policy indicates that significant numbers of powerful actors within the national security bureaucracy were unwilling to accept the collapse and repudiation of the model to which they had been committed for a quarter of a century. Indeed, the paradigm continues to shape the relationship in powerful ways, despite Howard's strategic retreat to the safety of the US Alliance. An opportunity to influence the future political development of the Indonesian republic is slipping away because of apparent resistance in Foreign Affairs to forcing the pace on the prosecution for war crimes of senior Indonesian military figures.

In May this year, a former army intelligence officer accused the Australian government of suppressing information about a large massacre of between fifty and two hundred East Timorese at the Maliana police station in 1999. Survivors later spoke of how a ring of TNI and armed police formed an outer cordon around a group of militia who then hacked their victims to death with machetes. Captain Andrew Plunkett of the parachute battalion alleged to the SBS *Dateline* program that Canberra had advance warning of a planned massacre in the police station in Maliana, but refused to pass the information on to the UN, which advised independence supporters to seek shelter there during post-ballot violence. Plunkett also said that Australian troops who inspected the scene had orders 'to minimise estimates of the death toll' and 'go lightly' on the issue of TNI body disposal. Plunkett said Australia received good intelligence of a plan to round up and kill independence supporters in Maliana, but the reports were 'pushed up the chain of command, hosed down and politically wordsmithed by the Asia division of the Department of Foreign Affairs and Trade'.

Wayne Sievers, a former Australian Federal Police Officer who tried to warn the UN in East Timor of the planned atrocity before it was put into action, told of pressure from Foreign Affairs staffers to downplay the participation of TNI personnel. Sievers had obtained intelligence detailing extensive links between militia and the TNI. An informant within Maliana's pro-Indonesian militia told him of a meeting he attended with other senior militia figures, Indonesian government officials and military officers, at which the post-ballot execution of the town's pro-independence campaigners was plotted. The UN dismissed Siever's report and the Australian Foreign Affairs officer to whom he reported refused to follow through on the police officer's warnings.

Sievers told *Dateline*:

> He refused to come to my house to take it. It was at that stage that the warning light went on and I thought, 'These guys already know and they don't want any more information that would be unwelcome news because there's a line here that the Government has taken or a position that the Government has got itself into, that it can't extract itself from.' So it doesn't want to hear the bad news or the contrary news, so it can claim ignorance at the end of the day, if indeed the whole thing turns bad. That's what I believe happened.

Sievers was made to understand that no paper trail should be left to implicate the TNI or to hint at Australian knowledge of its complicity. Foreign Minister Downer seemed distressed when confronted by the allegations, denying that any Australian government would have any truck with protecting war criminals. He was at some pains, however, to point out that as minister he could not know what happened in every police station or behind every tree in Timor. Despite Downer's affront, the fact remains that apart from pro forma gestures such as calling for the prosecution of those responsible for atrocities – the diplomatic equivalent of calling for an end to world hunger – serious logistic support for Indonesia's beleaguered Human Rights Commission and the UN's investigative apparatus has been withheld. Not only has signals intelligence been denied to investigators, but as both Plunkett and Sievers make clear, any activity aimed at embarrassing figures such as Wiranto or Zacky Anwar has been stymied from Canberra.

Again, the situation is not a simple matter of a monolithic bureaucracy applying unstated policy. There are, as there have always been, serious fractures within the bureaucracy over management of the Indonesian relationship. The most damaging leaks, such as those from the Defence Intelligence Organisation that confirmed Australian knowledge of TNI responsibility for violence in East Timor, have come from within the military and intelligence complex, which has abandoned Woolcott's Kissingerian realism with much greater alacrity than their colleagues in Foreign Affairs. Having to face down the proxies of the TNI in September '99 probably helped with the change of heart. Orwell's words concerning W. H. Auden come to mind again: such amorality is only possible if you are always somewhere else when the trigger is pulled.

The 'hard-headed' realism of Australian foreign policy was always based on being somewhere else. As a putative reading of power politics, however, it has left much to be desired. Woolcott was not wrong to oppose that course of reasoning which constructed the question of East Timor and the overarching relationship in moral terms. He was right to push the view that his responsibility was to Australia's future, not East Timor's. He was grievously mistaken in assuming this future would be secured through *détente* with a corrupt dictatorship. The hard heads and realists were guilty of a mortal sin by their own reckoning. In both 1975 and 1999, they proved themselves completely unrealistic – wedded to desire and not cold calculation.

The question of war crimes is looming as a new touchstone for Australian realism. Once more it seems that the hollow promise of gaining advantage from an alliance with powerful interests has blinded Canberra to the alternate prescription of a truly hard-headed approach. For while ministers and their ALP shadows consistently talk about a new partnership with a democratic Indonesia, they ignore the fact that such a democracy is a weak, endangered concept with only a few genuine supporters among the ruling elites of the archipelago. Indonesian democracy is assailed by many foes, but few more threatening than the military and its commercial and political allies. If the senior officers who planned and executed the ethnic cleansing of East Timor are allowed to go free – and some have even been promoted – it is a laydown certainty that they will employ the same black arts against the population of Aceh, the Moluccas, West Irian and finally metropolitan Java itself. Removing them through the agency of a war crimes tribunal would curtail their ability to persecute reformers and interfere with the development of a true civil society.

It is certainly the case that pushing for such a tribunal, or offering material support to those Indonesians who are attempting to throw off the crushing weight of a collapsed dictatorship, will further degrade an already damaged relationship. But attempting to re-establish a close connection with the very same forces that brought Indonesia to calamity and would do so again is not a very realistic prescription for securing Australia's strategic future.

Some myths are best dealt with early. Despite the frisson of dread which ran through the Australian polity in the darkest days of the East Timor crisis, the Indonesian armed forces do not pose a mortal threat to this country, menacing as they may have seemed. They have never posed a serious threat to Australia, and were an adventurist regime in Jakarta to launch a military build-up tomorrow, they would need well over a decade to put in place a force projection capability with any realistic hope of defeating the Australian Defence Force in a general war. Even though the borders of the two countries are so close, their actual population and pro-duction centres are far removed, with Jakarta twice as far from Sydney as London is from Istanbul. The Indonesian military build-up required to create a force capable of acting at such a distance would be so massive an undertaking that it simply could not be kept secret. A regional arms race would ensue, with Singapore and Malaysia leading the way. Through its alliance with the US, Australia enjoys first-class intelligence capabilities and would have many years advance warning of an emerging threat. (Whether the ascendant theology of Foreign Affairs acknowledged that threat would be a different matter, of course). Notwithstanding Australia's relatively small population, the nation's security rests upon a number of comparative strategic advantages: an advanced industrial base, strong social cohesion and relatively sophisticated defence forces which are already exploiting the so-called revolution in military affairs through their alliance with the US. With the Howard Government's recent defence spending initiative, and with the effects of the Asian economic meltdown still crippling Indonesian government spending, the capability gap will only grow in the next decade.

Indeed, given present force structures and doctrine, Indonesia would have some claim to being a little put out by the popular perception of it as a threat to Australia. The Australian Defence Force has long been trained and equipped to fight high-intensity wars alongside US forces at some distance from the Australian mainland. Even with the rhetorical shift to defence self-reliance in the last decade, Australian military doctrine still speaks openly of threats arising within the Indonesian archipelago or transiting through it, and Australian forces have been structured with this in mind. The ADF – primarily the Navy and the RAAF – maintain the capacity and assert the right to launch attacks on hostile forces to the north. The reverse is not true of the Indonesian Armed Forces.

Since the arrival of the New Order, the Indonesian military has always looked inwards for threats to national survival. The army is many times larger than the air force and navy – the two services most needed to threaten adversaries outside the country's borders. In that sense, the structure of the TNI is almost the inverse of the ADF, which has allowed its army to run down while pouring resources into expensive long-range weapons platforms such as submarines, guided missile frigates and strategic strike aircraft. The acquisition of AWACS aircraft in the near future will further extend the RAAF's superiority over Indonesia's air force, and while President Wahid has announced a modest program of naval expansion, most of the money will go towards increasing the capacity of the TNI to deploy marine forces within the archipelago against groups like the Free Aceh Movement. At the moment, Indonesia's navy is crippled, with at best only 25 per cent of its ships operational.

Moreover, the vast size of the Indonesian army belies a structural weakness which renders it much less threatening than it might otherwise appear. Of about 230 000 personnel, most are comparatively poorly trained, ill-equipped and often undisciplined territorial forces such as East Timor's Battalion 745. They can boast world's best practice in the highly competitive field of terrorising unarmed, illiterate peasants, but their claims to wider military competence are questionable. The Army's professional core consists of the two light infantry divisions that make up the Strategic Command or *Kostrad* and the four disgraced special forces units of *Kopassus*, a total of about 35 000 men, similar in size to the regular army and reserve forces of Australia. Indonesia is a poor, underdeveloped country with 17 000 islands to protect and a history of simmering, occasionally frightful internecine conflicts. From the earliest days of the republic, the armed forces, and in particular the army, have seen their mission less in terms of deterring external aggression than in binding up the archipelago's hundreds of micro-nationalist strands into one Indonesian identity. With defence self-reliance an economic impossibility, ABRI adopted a philosophy of 'total people's defence', with the entire population mobilised into a citizen's militia to grind down any invading force.

The terror campaign in East Timor – and doubtless its descendant in West Papua should the independence movement there ever prove more than a distraction – was thus no aberration. It sat comfortably within a strategy that has long had the formal imprimatur of the Indonesian state, even if in this case it was a freelance effort of the military acting against the wishes of President Habibie's barely legitimate interim government. Militia such as *Aitarak*, Team Alpha and *Besi Merah Putih* are an integral part of Indonesian defence strategy. Since independence they have been seen as the people's army, with which the territorial battalions and the central command have been expected to work. Endless speculation on the role of the state in their creation and control completely misses the point that they are not independent entities. They are organs of the military and ultimately the republic. They are also, it goes without saying, of negligible strategic importance to Australia – even if the militia in West Timor are of immediate operational concern to Australian forces on the border.

Australian planners are rightly more concerned with the political threat from the TNI and associated nationalist forces, which have been incensed by the Howard Government's role in prising away the 27th Province. Despite – or perhaps because of – Australian diplomatic efforts to forestall the issue of independent peace-keepers before the ballot, many in Indonesia feel betrayed by their erstwhile friend. This endless cycle of disappointment is almost a defining characteristic of long-term transactions between the two countries. Like the generals of '75, senior figures currently in the Indonesian military and government cannot understand how, having been so supportive of Indonesia's difficulties in the former Portuguese colony, Australia could suddenly turn on them and lead the charge into Dili. Once again, this outcome was predicted by the losers of the debate in 1975, who argued that a policy response lacking authentic and widespread domestic support, while endurable in the short term, was unsustainable over the long arc, and that any future reversal would only serve to upset the Indonesians more than an immediate lack of support. One wonders whether the hard significance of this lesson is causing many sleepless nights among the Foreign Affairs staff responsible for policy on West Irian.

It is undeniable that the once-close relationship with Indonesia has been sundered. The intimacy which marked the Keating prime ministership is gone, replaced by suspicion and hostility, and commentators like Woolcott and Keating himself make a valid point when they argue that Australia has lost a valuable supporter in the region. It is now infinitely more difficult to negotiate the treacherous shoals of regional politics with both Jakarta and Kuala Lumpur playing payback. Arguably, however, the tragedy lies not in the outcome, but in its predictability.

At one level, Keating's policy of Asian engagement was an admirable break with the pattern of the past. It represented a quantum leap from previous, far-sighted diplomatic initiatives from both sides of politics, such as the rapprochement with Japan and the enlightened humanism of the Columbo Plan under Menzies' Foreign Minister Richard Casey, and the recognition of China by Gough Whitlam. In fact, it is one of the small ironies of this story that two of our most unsympathetic occupants of the Lodge are worthy of some sympathy, or at least understanding, for the different ways in which they attempted to deal with the conundrum of Indonesia under wildly different circumstances; Paul Keating through engagement and John Howard through divorce.

When Keating assumed the prime minister's office, the Gordian knot of our tangled relationship had just been snarled even further by the massacre at Santa Cruz. Gareth Evans missed the Caucus vote that ended Bob Hawke's term because he was in Jakarta, representing Australia's displeasure at the massacre. Keating – who has written that he was not prepared 'to let the whole of our complex relationship with 210 million people [be] subject to this one issue' – decided to cut through the knot. Jakarta would be the first foreign capital he would visit as prime minister. There had been no direct contact between the two nations' heads of government for nearly a decade, a situation which he thought 'extraordinary between two neighbours'. And he was right.

Keating's policy of Asian engagement was altogether commendable, and his particular emphasis on repairing the link to Jakarta was faultless – from an aspirational point of view. The institutional architecture which he, Evans, Ali Alatas and Suharto put in place consisted of exactly the sort of ties that should exist between neighbouring states which want to work for each other's benefit rather than against each other's interests. The high-level councils, the frequent ministerial visits, the programmed exchanges of students, journalists and business people established the pattern you want to see in transactions between two geographically contiguous but culturally remote societies. In spite of their demonisation by some supporters of East Timorese independence, Keating and Evans were honourable men attempting to do their best by their country. Standing amidst the wreckage of their strategy, however, we look down and see that it was constructed on a foundation of ash and bones.

Although Keating was correct about the necessity for engagement with Indonesia, he was entirely wrong in assuming it was sustainable. His major published exposition on the topic, *Engagement: Australia Faces the Asia-Pacific*, is strangely conflicted because of this. In the chapter devoted to Indonesia, he acknowledges the faults of the Suharto regime and the systemic contradictions which led to its demise. Furthermore, he gives the impression of having been aware of such problems while formulating his policy of strategic frottage. 'The consistent message of all the Australian official briefing I was receiving through that period,' he says, 'was that the

New Order institutions were coming under strain, that criticism of Suharto and his family would grow, but that he was likely to be in power until at least the 1998 election.' Keating says that his aim was to use his rapport with Suharto to 'develop structural changes that would outlast us both'. In relation to the most controversial of all those changes, the 1995 Agreement on Maintaining Security, he wrote that Suharto was the only person capable of delivering such an accord within Indonesia.

If this was so, what on earth made Keating assume it would survive the old dictator's passing? He admits that Suharto himself was forced to intervene 'in support of the relationship' when 'some of his more hot-headed officials' went ballistic over Australia's bungled rejection of proposed Ambassador General Herman Mantiri in mid-1995. While Keating and Evans were busily thickening up the ties, they ignored the obvious fact that, much as they might wish to avoid hanging the entire relationship from the single thread of Timor, that thread remained the central thing around which all other engagement grew. Keating admits as much when he insists that both he and Evans made constant representations to Jakarta over the disputed territory, attempting to make the Indonesian government understand that a militarised solution was untenable. If the impossibility of Indonesian victory over the East Timorese was accepted in Canberra, and the growing instability of the Suharto regime was projected into the medium-term future, why could nobody see that the centrifugal political energies which were emerging all over the world would also play themselves out in Indonesia. One assumes this is the reason we keep strategic analysts on the public payroll.

Elsewhere in *Engagement*, Keating delivers a caustic diagnosis of the fractures then undermining the regime, the rapacious corruption of Suharto's family and their feudal business associates, and the contending forces which would soon openly assail it. He was not blind to the dangers ahead. In one of his most damning critiques, he writes that Suharto failed to understand the ways his own administration had transformed Indonesian society, with economic development requiring political change that the President and the New Order were completely incapable of delivering, given that it would mean their own negation.

> He failed to respond to the demands of richer, better educated people for more control over their own lives. The commercial activities of his family and friends distorted the economy and undermined his legacy. Committed from his revolutionary days to a united, secular Indonesia, he could not bring himself to change a harsh and unworkable policy in East Timor. He was for keeping an archipelago and a nation together at all costs. And the costs were high for others and also for him.

Keating points out, and it should acknowledged, that set against Suharto's miserable human rights record, hundreds of millions of Indonesians benefited directly from the sustained economic growth of his era. Per capita income increased more than ten-fold between 1970 and 1997. The proportion of Indonesians living in absolute poverty (not the infinitely more comfortable, welfare-supported poverty we are familiar with) declined from about three-quarters of the population to 11 per cent just prior to the meltdown. Paul Keating's blind spot was exposed, however, when he said of Santa Cruz that it was 'an appalling lapse of control by individual security forces on the ground in Dili rather than deliberate policy instruction from Jakarta'. In fact, Santa Cruz stood as a talisman for everything that was wrong with the New Order, not just in Timor, but generally. While there may not have been a specific order sent from Jakarta, the survivor accounts make it clear that there was no 'appalling lapse of control'. Far from it. The actions of the Indonesian military that occasion – controlled, premeditated, inexorable and totally without remorse – were consistent with long-established methods of regime maintenance both in the former Portuguese colony and throughout the nation. Similar tactics were filling mass graves in Aceh at the same time.

Bob Lowry, quoting Harold Crouch, says 'it was a "disguised coup" in 1966 which put Suharto in power and it was the armed forces which kept him there until the very end.' The routine resort to state terror characterised the New Order government from its earliest moments to its death rattle on the streets of Jakarta in 1998, with the army turning its guns on the sons and daughters of the Javanese middle classes. As Dr Stephen Sherlock of the Parliamentary Library's Foreign Affairs, Defence and Trade Group wrote in April 1999, the violent downfall of Suharto was an indication of fundamental weaknesses within the political structure he had created.

> The crisis also revealed what many people had been arguing for many years, that the New Order's economic achievements had come at the price of political repression which had suffocated the growth of healthy political institutions. Dominated by the personality of President Soeharto, the New Order silenced voices of opposition and reduced parliament, the judiciary and the press to the tools of the president. The Armed Forces were relied upon to prevent any expression of the deep social, cultural and regional divisions in Indonesia. ABRI has also been accused of sometimes manipulating such divisions for political and financial gain. Freed of many of the restrictions of the New Order, many social divisions have now resurfaced in a violent and unpredictable way, as the disturbances in Ambon and Kalimantan have illustrated.

Suharto and his cohorts dominated every institution and process. The media was 'subject to often arbitrary and inconsistent censorship, with newspapers and magazines liable to sudden closure'. Sherlock described elections as nothing more than 'a ritual whose results were known well before they commenced', with only three parties vying for seats in an irrelevant parliament dominated as a matter of course by the official party, *Golkar*, which ran the machinery of the state in lockstep with the military, under ABRI's 'dual function'. The civilian, military and political administration were thus all entwined and supportive of each other. The territorial structure of the army, with military officers occupying positions from hamlet to Cabinet, ensured that no refuge from state surveillance and retribution existed for anyone who stood against the New Order.

In the end, for all its material achievements, the power of the regime was based not on the consent of the governed, but on their terror and submission. Richard Tanter identifies three types of state terror that buttressed Suharto's rule; the 'constitutive terror' of 1965–66 which was the foundation of the New Order; peripheral terror in the outer provinces where separatist movements threatened the unitary state; and intermittent, targeted terror in the metropolitan centre itself. The kidnapping and torture of student democracy activists by special forces under the command of Suharto's son-in-law, Prabowo Subianto, was an example of the latter. Other victims over the years included Islamic activists, labour organisers and even thousands of criminals in the early 1980s. On each occasion the regime returned to its roots. Not simply content to eliminate opposition or competitors or inconvenient former allies, the bodies of the chosen were usually laid out in public spaces, where they might serve to induce an exemplary, generalised terror among other deserving targets and the wider population.

There is a natural and inevitably fatal flaw in such regimes, and an inherent danger of close connection with them for countries such as Australia. The New Order could be variously described as authoritarian or totalitarian, depending on which area and at what time you were observing its activities. As a general principle, the further from Jakarta, the more repressive and intolerant its rule was. The Republic of Indonesia was created out of the administrative fiction of a former European empire which has itself long since vanished from the earth. The Dutch built their colony on the bones of a Javanese empire, and the story of Indonesia since independence can partly be told as the struggle of a Java-centric administration to bind hundreds of disparate cultures, language groups and ethnic blocs to an imagined national destiny. Some allegiance was owed to that vision because of the achievements of the New Order in social and economic development. But resistance was generated by the regime's grossly inequitable distribution of the rewards that came from development. The crucial point about Suharto's ultimate lack of legitimacy was not his resort to terror, but what that terror was protecting: massive, institutionalised corruption which, for all the vaunted economic growth of the Suharto era, saw the theft of billions of dollars of public assets, the debauching of the state for private ends and the enrichment of the centre at the expense of the periphery, and a comparatively small elite at the expense of hundreds of millions of Indonesian citizens.

Or perhaps subjects might be a better term. For the New Order was an imperial regime in all but name; a personalised despotism, with one man and his family at the apex and all of the resources of the state beholden to him, his palace guard and a corporate oligarchy of feudal lords. The rapacious greed of the first family and their courtiers is only a little less fantastic than the aplomb with which they have dodged attempts to retrieve the loot for the public good. The family established monopolies in a vast range of goods, backed by the power of the state, for the benefit of both clan and cronies. Hundreds of nominally charitable foundations called *Yayasans* extorted donations from public and private enterprise as a matter of law, with legislation passed making such donations compulsory. State companies were hijacked by sons and daughters, most often by being forced into joint ventures with Suharto family companies. As Dr George Aditjondro explains, 'This pattern was often repeated over the years, enabling the Suharto children to build their television stations, toll roads, telecommunications networks, supermarkets and other businesses with the minimum capital and little or no competition at all from similar companies.' The military was intimately entwined in the process through its own bogus charities, such as the Kobame Foundation of the special forces (*Kopassus*),

> which owns the new Graha Cijantung shopping mall on Kopassus land at their Cijantung headquarters south of Jakarta, [as well as] part-ownerships in the Horizon Hotel in Jakarta and a timber concession in Kalimantan, a methanol distribution agency from the

state oil mining company, Pertamina, a Java–Sumatra shipping line, and a coal bricket company partly owned by Suharto's eldest son, Sigit Harjojudanto.

Substantial as *Kopassus*'s business interests may seem, they are dwarfed by the gargantuan wealth of other military commercial concerns. Crucially, these connections, most of which did not perish with the formal end of the regime, now act to secure Suharto against the depredations of reformers, as surviving institutions such as the TNI and their allied business combines manoeuvre to secure their own interests. This pirate cabal is composed of the same figures who were responsible for running up huge levels of foreign debt to fund a boom in the construction of holiday resorts, golf courses, hotels and unleaseable office blocks which undermined the rupiah in the crash of '97. This in a country which was still fundamentally poor. By way of contrast, before the crash the Australian economy was twice the size of Indonesia's, despite being based on a population roughly one-tenth the size. The glittering, Manhattanised skyline of Jakarta, which so impressed foreign capital markets for at least a short time, was paid for by tens of millions of Indonesians subsisting in relative impoverishment in resource-rich areas such as Aceh and West Irian.

The uncertain, reactive embrace of regional devolution by the Wahid government is not likely to do anything to alleviate deep-rooted tensions arising from decades of inequity and repression. While the headline actors of the New Order may be gone, the underlying interests remain and cannot allow an authentic transfer of authority to take place because it would mean an enormous and probably fatal surrender of wealth and power on their part. It is also possible that empowering the regions may well mean empowering the very separatist energies against which the centre has fought for so long. There is a point at which so much blood has been spilt there is no hope of redemption. The lesson of East Timor is that violence does not destroy nationalism, but rather creates it.

The flaw at the heart of the New Order was its irreducible corruption and barbarism. The defining characteristic of dictatorships is that they dictate. They have a mania for control which will allow of no challenge, legitimate or otherwise. It is why they so often abruptly mutate from apparently stable states into chaos and madness; because, try as they might, the ruling autocracy simply cannot control everything. While a balance of purchased allegiance and terrorised obedience can maintain a regime for decades, underlying pressures are not addressed, simply choked off at some point where they build up awaiting a rupture. Eventually, inevitably, fate will conspire to present the regime with a set of circumstances it cannot control. For the Soviet Union it was a renewed arms race which bankrupted the eastern bloc. For China it will probably come from the forces unleashed by the economic liberalisation the Communist Party has encouraged in a desperate bid to safeguard itself. For Suharto and the New Order it was the meltdown of 1997. The tsunami which roared out of north-east Asia simply rolled over the pathetic, jury-rigged defences that Suharto's hand-picked Cabinet of family members and favoured spivs had erected to protect their monopolies and shake-down rackets. So complete was the shift in sentiment away from them that not even Prabowo's manufactured terror could stem the tide.

A defining paradox of modern post-industrial democracy is a complex plurality of rival but complementary power centres. Mature democracies vest power not just in executive political authority, but in a myriad of social, economic and cultural institutions, all of which stand as alternative sources of legitimate authority. Stakeholders in mature democracies understand that because power is not unitary and fixed in a rigid hierarchy, most often bonded to an individual at the summit, the loss of autonomy in one area, even of executive state power, does not imply a mortal threat to any other interests, including economic ones, which they might hold.

Executive power in mature democracies is cyclic, and to lose power in an election simply means preparing to regain it at a later date. In a federal democracy such as Australia's, with different levels of government-assigned responsibilities, it is likely that parties will hold executive power at one level but not at another. More importantly, however, they are not the only actors. Millions of individuals, acting singly or as part of social and economic bodies as diverse as the board of Westpac or a suburban residents' action group, retain for themselves significant capacities to act for their own benefit.

Despite the forced resignation of Suharto and the implementation of multiparty elections in Indonesia, democracy there remains fragile. The structures and institutions that have evolved in the west over thousands of years, and to which deep cultural allegiance is owed, do not yet exist in the archipelago. The institutions and power blocs that presently hold or contend for effective power, and upon which the unity of Indonesia rests, are components of the same disgraced establishment that underpinned the New Order regime. The pillars of that regime, *Golkar* and the bureaucracy, the crony capital establishment and the armed forces, are now fractured and beset by such emerging players as student activists, Islamic organisations, regional independence movements and a shattered but still sizeable urban middle class and working class. But the Indonesian polity has not evolved in response because it does not yet have the capacity to evolve. Under Suharto, potentially competing power centres were either co-opted or repressed. No tradition existed of cyclic transfer of power or of acceptance of non-state authority – the prerequisites of a modern democratic state. Power was fixed and unitary. Latent competitors were enmeshed in a mutually supporting network of corrupt business and political arrangements. But because there was no alternative to dictatorial rule, the millions of stakeholders occupying those various power centres had no chance to develop an allegiance to an overarching system in which the distribution of rewards and security was accepted as fair. The New Order was, like all dictatorships, an all-or-nothing proposition. You either came on board for the big win or, in the final extremity, you dug yourself a shallow grave.

The aftermath can be observed in the ferocity of the many contested transitions which have occurred or are taking place. Because the Indonesian state under the New Order had neither the experience nor the ability to negotiate transfers of power, status and wealth with domestic competitors, it guaranteed that all such demands would be seen as wrongful and as a threat to the regime, although this was always expressed as a threat to the unity of the state itself. The violence of Suharto's fall, the weakness of the administrations that have followed his, and the disaster in East Timor, all lend credence to this thesis. An imperious tyranny which came to power in one of the premier bloodbaths of the twentieth century, and ultimately guaranteed its hold on power with state terror, could not be expected to lay solid foundations for succession. Indonesia's two hundred and ten million citizens thus find themselves not so much repressed by a new system as trapped under the wreckage of an old one.

Trapped, too, is Australia. All of the oft-stated truisms about the consequence of geography remain valid. There are many points at which the interests of the two nations will either coincide or collide, and the promotion of Australia's regional claims can still be greatly improved by a friendly and co-operative partnership with Jakarta – the sort of partnership which is so obviously absent at the moment. However, the lessons of Timor should not be forgotten, if they were ever learned in the first place.

Wishful thinking is no substitute for cold realism. It is one of the abiding ironies of the last quarter-century that the least realistic and in some ways the most romantic view of Indonesian policy held sway in Canberra. Australia had very little direct influence over Indonesian state action in its disputed province and retains none over strategy and tactics in other troubled areas such as West Irian. When framing Australian policy, the question should always be asked, what is sustainable over the very long term? The answers will not necessarily provide short-term comfort, but they might just help avoid creating a situation where, once again, a regime in Jakarta feels justifiably betrayed by the apparent skittishness of its southern neighbour. Australian governments can run the relationship without reference to wider community concerns for limited periods of time. But if we treat with a violent, repressive oligarchy, there will come a reckoning at some future point. Until the level of understanding between the two countries vastly improves, and there is an acceptance of fundamental differences, a fatal flaw lies at the heart of any state-to-state relationship that attempts to move beyond merely practical shared concerns.

Much as the Department of Foreign Affairs and Trade would love to be left alone to reconstruct the relationship as they think best, they cannot operate without reference to some base level of public assent. On any given day the electorate is most likely to be profoundly uninterested in foreign policy, but there does come a point at which their lack of engagement ceases, their minds and more importantly their passions are aroused, and at that time no government can hope to make policy in the quiet cloisters of some diplomatic arcadia. If they wish to survive as a government, they will have no choice but to prosecute the issue in line with popular feeling, as distasteful and inconvenient as that almost always proves to be.

No settlement of Indonesia's future has been reached, or likely will be in the near term. But the chances are slim of an orderly passage to some form of benign, multicultural, free market democracy. The persistence of an informal power structure based on the remains of the New Order, with elements competing against each other and against the formal structure of the state itself, is an assurance of turmoil. The decaying but animated corpse of the old system is abroad in the land and it may well have the best prospects of all the forces competing for control of the archipelago. The attempted embrace of martial law by President Wahid when faced with serious political challenges in May this year demonstrated just how weak the commitment to the rule of law and liberal forms was, even in the case of one of the republic's leading liberals. Little succour can be taken from the Indonesian military's refusal to back Wahid's attempt at executive rebellion. While couched in reassuring rhetoric about the military's commitment to democratic reform, in truth it had more to do with the military's commitment to Wahid's removal.

It is heresy to say so, but for as long as Indonesia remains an unstable and potentially authoritarian state, elemental political differences will inevitably preclude a close and abiding relationship. That is not to say that Australia can or should disengage entirely. There are some simple and relatively inexpensive options for any government that wants to pursue constructive dialogue and act to influence, if only in a small way, the development of a civic culture in Indonesia. Educational aid, support for institution-building, especially in areas such as the judiciary, and meaningful cultural and business exchanges could all be usefully expanded. But, difficult as it might make our diplomats' lives in the immediate future, no administration in Jakarta should ever again be allowed to assume that it will have Australian support, tacit or otherwise, when it turns the machinery of oppression on its own people.

SOURCES

Introduction

I am grateful to William Maley for highlighting the pertinence of George Orwell's remark about chaps who always seem to be somewhere else when the going gets sticky.

The Dogs of Los Palos

The hard work of tracing Battalion 745's exit from East Timor was not mine but the *Christian Science Monitor*'s Cameron Barr. Supplementary colour was provided by Norman Lewis, as indicated in the text, and the writers of Lonely Planet, whose guide to Indonesia provided useful background information. The events listed as occurring on September 9 were all taken from the ABC's chronology of the East Timor crisis, available on the broadcaster's website. Other media reports quoted in the text, such as Keith Richburg's *Washington Post* article, were accessed through the website of the East Timor Action Network [etan.org]. Details of militia activity were taken from reports by Amnesty International [amnesty.org] and the Carter Foundation [cartercenter.org].

James Dunn's report on the complicity of the TNI in militia violence was provided by the *Sydney Morning Herald* at their website [smh.com.au]. The report of the Indonesian Human Rights Commission (KPP HAM) is available at various sites online. I took mine from etan.org.

The specifications of the ASLAV are given on the Australian Army's home page [army.gov.au], as are some details of the confrontation between 2 Cav and the Brave Ones on September 21. These latter can be found in a speech given by Peter Cosgrove, archived on his home page within the army site. Bob Breene also described that event and he, along with Cosgrove, is my major source for the encounter.

Champions of the Overdog

The details of Richard Woolcott's many postings are taken from the

Department of Foreign Affairs and Trade's documentary history, *Australia and the Incorporation of Portuguese Timor 1974–76*. This collection is the major source for this chapter, containing as it does the raw material of Australian diplomatic manoeuvres during that crucial period.

The information used in the Santa Cruz section comes from five main sources. Alan Nairn's testimony to the US Senate Committee on Foreign Relations on February 17, 1992 is available at: http://bsd.mojones.com/east_timor/evidence/nairn.html. Amy Goodman's narrative can be read at: http://www.lbbs.org/ZMag/articles/. She provided much of the information about the human rights campaign that emerged in America after Santa Cruz.

Further details were extracted from 'East Timor's Unfinished Struggle: Inside the Timorese Resistance' by Constancio Pinto and Matthew Jardine, available at http://zena.secureforum.com/Znet/ZMag/articles/dec96timor.htm. It includes a contribution by Nairn that is the source for my remarks about official US reluctance to abandon Jakarta after the massacre.

The quote from Try Sutrisno is taken from the article 'East Timor: A People Shattered By Lies and Silence' by Prof. Antonio Barbedo de Magalhaes, which I originally accessed through the etan.org site. It is, however, widely available online. It is also the source of the story about Henry Kissinger's ambush by Alan Nairn.

Finally, anyone seeking to research the reaction of the New Order to the Santa Cruz aftermath could profitably seek out an article called 'News From Nowhere' by Loren Ryter from the ANU Soc.Sci.WWW Server at http://coombs.anu.edu.au.

As already mentioned, the primary source for data about Australian government policy in 1974–6 is the DFAT collection. However, a useful summary of the events leading up to the invasion is found in the opening chapter of *Death In Balibo, Lies in Canberra* and I also drew on that while trying to organise the events of the period in my mind. Woolcott's speech to the New Zealand Institute of International Affairs is reproduced in *East Timor – The Consequences*.

Details of ABRI and TNI atrocities in East Timor from 1975–1999 are so widely available it begs the question of how Australian policy officers managed to ignore them over the years. John Taylor's book, *Indonesia's Forgotten War: The Hidden History of East Timor*, and James Dunn's *Timor: A People Betrayed*, are two of the most significant collations. Aditjondro's description of the 'Fence of Legs' can be found in 'Ninjas, Nanggalas, Monuments and Mossad Manuals: An Anthropology of Indonesian State Terror in East Timor', in Jeff Sluka (ed.), *Death Squad: The Anthropology of State Terror*.

Murray Edelman advances his theories of political mythology in *Politics as Symbolic Action*, but they have been so widely accepted and built on by other researchers over the last thirty years that I don't suppose he can claim ownership anymore. I still like to steal my ideas from the guy who came up with them, though. And Edelman is is the inspiration, if not the direct source, for much of the discussion about the bureaucratic psychology of DFAT.

The details of accusations that Australia is continuing to to cover up TNI atrocities can be read at the *Dateline* homepage on the SBS website. A transcript of the entire show is available.

End of Empire

I am indebted to Bob Lowry for his research into the capabilities and doctrine of the TNI and its predecessor, ABRI. You can read his thought on the matter at the website of the Australian Parliamentary Library [aph.gov.au/library.pubs]. The Centre for Strategic and International Studies provided some supporting data on the current readiness of the TNI [csis.org].

Aditjondro's analysis of Suharto's wealth and the New Order is widely available online, but can best be accessed through his own page at the University of Newcastle.

BIBLIOGRAPHY

Akashi, Yoji., *The East Timor Question in Australian–Indonesia Relations, 1974–78: An Australian Perception*, Centre for Australian Studies, Nanzan University, Nagoya, Japan, 1995.

Australian Institute of International Affairs, *The East Timor Crisis: Implications and Lessons: Summary Report*, Canberra, 1999.

Ball, D. & McDonald, H., *Death in Balibo, Lies in Canberra*, Allen and Unwin, Sydney, 2000.

Bell, C., 'East Timor, Canberra and Washington: A Case Study in Crisis Management', Australian Institute of International Affairs, V. 54, No. 2, 2000, pp.171–176.

Breene, B., *Mission Accomplished East Timor*, Allen and Unwin, Sydney, 2001.

Brown, B. (ed.), *East Timor – The Consequences*, New Zealand Institute of International Affairs, Wellington, 2000.

Budiman, A., Hatley, B. & Kingsbury, D., *Reformasi – Crisis and Change in Indonesia*, Monash Asia Institute, Clayton, 1999.

Callinan, Sir Bernard, *Independent Company: the Australian Army in Portuguese Timor 1941–43*, Heinemann, Richmond, Vic., 1984.

Catley, B. & Dugis, V., *Australian Indonesian Relations Since 1945: The Garuda and the Kangaroo*, Ashgate, Aldershot, Hants, England; Brookfield, Vt., 1998.

Cobb, A., 'East Timor and Australia's Security Role: Issues and Scenarios', Dept. of the Parliamentary Library, Information and Research Services, Canberra, 1999.

Cobb, A. & Frost, F., 'The Future of East Timor: Major Current Issues',
Dept. of the Parliamentary Library, Information and Research Services,
Foreign Affairs, Defence and Trade Group, Canberra, 1999.

Cotton, J. (ed.), *East Timor and Australia: AIIA Contributions to the Policy Debate*,
Australian Defence Studies Centre, ADFA, Canberra, 1999.

Department of Foreign Affairs and Trade, *Australia and the Indonesian Incorporation
of Portuguese Timor 1974–1976*, Melb. University Press, Melbourne, 2000.

Dunn, J., *Timor: A People Betrayed*, ABC Books, Sydney, 1996.

Edelman, M., *Politics as Symbolic Action*, Markham, Chicago, 1971.

Hill, H., *The Indonesian Economy in Crisis: Causes, Consequences and Lessons*, Allen &
Unwin, St. Leonards, N.S.W., 1999.

Kammen, D. & Siddharth C., *A Tour of Duty: Changing Patterns of Military Politics in
Indonesia in the 1990s*, Cornell Modern Indonesia Project, Ithaca, N.Y., 1999.

Keating, P., *Engagement: Australia Faces the Asia-Pacific*, Macmillan, Sydney, 2000.

Lewis, N., *An Empire of the East: Travels in Indonesia*, Jonathan Cape, London, 1993.

Lloyd, G., 'Indonesia's Future Prospects: Separatism, Decentralisation and
the Survival of the Unitary State', Dept. of the Parliamentary Library,
Information and Research Services, Foreign Affairs, Defence and Trade
Group, Canberra, 2000.

Lowry, B., 'Indonesian Armed Forces (Tentara Nasional Indonesia – TNI)',
Dept. of the Parliamentary Library, Information and Research Services,
Foreign Affairs, Defence and Trade Group, Canberra, 1999.

Lowry, B., 'Indonesia: Political Futures and Regional Security', Australian Defence Studies Centre, Canberra, 1999.

Lowry, B., 'Indonesian Defence and Security 2019', Australian Defence Studies Centre, Canberra, 1996.

Maley, W., 'Australia and the East Timor Crisis: Some Critical Comments', Australian Institute of International Affairs, V. 54, No. 2, 2000, pp. 151–161.

Schwarz, A. & Paris, J., *The Politics of Post-Suharto Indonesia*, Council on Foreign Relations, Singapore, 1999.

Senate Standing Committee on Foreign Affairs and Defence, *The Human Rights and Conditions of the People of East Timor*, September, 1983, Australian Government Publishing Service, Canberra 1983.

Sherlock, S., 'After the Elections, After East Timor: What's Next for Indonesia?', Dept. of the Parliamentary Library, Information and Research Services, Foreign Affairs, Defence and Trade Group, Canberra, 1999.

Sluka, J. (ed.), *Death Squad: The Anthropology of State Terror*, University of Pennsylvania Press, Philadelphia, 2000.

Taylor, J., *Indonesia's Forgotten War: The Hidden History of East Timor*, Pluto Press, Sydney, 1991.

Woolcott, R., 'The Consequences of the Crisis over East Timor', in Brown, B. (ed.), *East Timor – The Consequences*, New Zealand Institute of International Affairs, Wellington, 2000.

Websites

http://coombs.anu.edu.au/CoombswebPages/Coombspapers.html
> 'Australian Perceptions and Indonesian Reality'. Lecture by Carlyle A. Thayer to the New Zealand Institute of International Affairs (Dunedin Branch), Hocken Hall, The University of Otago, Dunedin, May 12, 1988. Text located in <u>asian-studies-archives/indonesia-archives</u>.

<u>www.csis.org</u>
> 'Indonesia–Australia: Relations Moving from Bad to Worse'
> by Richard W. Baker
> 'Tragedy and Uncertainty for Some, Potential Benefits for Others'
> by Samantha F. Ravich
> 'Challenges to Indonesia's Democratic Consolidation '
> by Dewi Fortuna Anwar
> 'Indonesia's Muslim Divide: Past and Present'
> by Charles U. Zenzie

http//www.etan.org/news/2000a/3exec.htm
> Indonesian Human Rights Commission (KPP HAM) report

http://munindo.brd.de
> 'Chopping the Global Tentacles of the Suharto Oligarchy: Can Aotearoa (New Zealand) Lead The Way?'
> by Dr. George J. Aditjondro (University of Newcastle, Australia)

http://www.cdi.org/
> Indonesian Defense Forces (TNI)

<u>www.abc.net.au</u>
> A chronology of the East Timor crisis

<u>www.csmonitor.com/atcsmonitor/specials/timor/</u>
> The *Christian Science Monitor* – 'A Brutal Exit – Battalion 745'

CORRESPONDENCE

from Ron Brunton

In November 1997, Robert Manne and I discussed *Bringing them home*, the report of the inquiry into the 'stolen generations' undertaken by the Human Rights and Equal Opportunity Commission (HREOC). Manne conceded that it had serious weaknesses. But he also said I should not publish my planned critique, because it would provide 'the right' with ammunition they could use to dismiss the whole issue. Instead, I should aim to write a better history of Aboriginal child removals. This was what he was doing.

It was an astonishing request, made even more so by his acknowledgement that public opinion 'overwhelmingly accepted the truthfulness' of the report at the time (*In Denial*, p. 42). Someone who had once editorialised (*Quadrant*, December 1992) about the duty of intellectuals to influence the world 'by discrediting the false and advancing the true', was saying, in effect, that certain falsehoods should be allowed to stand for political reasons.

With the publication of Manne's essay, *In Denial: The Stolen Generations and the Right*, the situation has become more extraordinary. After all, individuals who have identified the failings of *Bringing them home* are not just those who can be dismissed as 'right-wing'. Last December, for instance, the *Australian Financial Review* published an article called 'A matter for history' by Bain Attwood – no friend of 'the right' – which also found serious fault with the report. So perhaps to avoid being criticised for remaining silent about a document whose defects have become increasingly apparent, Manne has temporarily put aside the task of writing his 'better history' and done just what he warned me against – he has publicly acknowledged that *Bringing them home* has major flaws.

But this has also placed him in an uncomfortable position. He has only recently extricated himself from the 'right-winger' smear himself, and even then, as recent *Overland* editorials indicate, not with complete success. Consequently, like the *nouveaux riches* who strongly denigrate those from whom they have risen, Manne seems keen to convince everyone that he retains no vestiges of his former self. No adjectives are spared in berating the wickedness and vacuity of 'the right', which is supposedly running an organised campaign to discredit *Bringing them home* and the 'stolen generations'. Unfortunately however, in attempting to protect himself against potential snipers from one direction, he has opened up a whole new avenue for attacks on his intellectual credibility. *In Denial* shows that he is indifferent to factual evidence, apparently believing that he can make reckless claims which are demonstrably false without being called to account.

My comments about *In Denial* are confined solely to statements which refer to me directly or by implication, and these cover only around 10 per cent of the essay. The remaining 90 per cent includes numerous significant falsehoods as well, but I leave these for others to address. In the interests of economy, I have not always provided the full context and references to support my statements. However, anyone wishing to verify what I have written can consult 'The False Scholarship Syndrome' on the IPA website (www.ipa.org.au), which contains a detailed point-by-point rebuttal of all the specific criticisms that Manne has made of my writings on the 'stolen generations'. The website also includes *Betraying the Victims* (IPA Backgrounder, February 1998), which is the most comprehensive critique of *Bringing them home* I have published.

Manne seems unwilling to accept that there could be any justification for the position I argued from the beginning – that in the long run a shoddy and intellectually dishonest report betrays the victims of a great injustice. He also seems unable to comprehend that an irresponsible document like *Bringing them home* can make it much more difficult for contemporary authorities to achieve a wise and humane balance in deciding what to do with Aboriginal children in situations of risk.

Manne accuses me of being disingenuous, maintaining that I was a pioneer for those who say that the 'stolen generations' issue is a hoax and that the children were 'rescued'. He claims that not only have I refused to oppose them, I have supposedly joined them 'in an orchestrated campaign' (p. 42). But as he must know, I have made it abundantly clear on many occasions that I am against those who think it is a 'hoax', and that I do not accept the notion of a 'rescued generation' (e.g. 'Dilemma in making amends', *Courier-Mail*, 4 September 1999; 'Justice O'Loughlin and *Bringing them home*', *Quadrant*, December 2000). Manne seems to think that speaking at a conference constitutes sharing a 'platform' with all other speakers (p. 42), irrespective of whether I agreed with their views or not. As well as casting a revealing light on his intolerance, these remarks would place me in the position of being a co-campaigner on Aboriginal issues with people such as Henry Reynolds and Aden Ridgeway, with whom I have also spoken on 'the same platform'.

Manne obviously believes my motives are unsavoury. 'Retained by a private enterprise think-tank supported by mining money' (p. 42), I have supposedly carved out a niche market attacking judgements or reports 'conspicuously sympathetic to the Aborigines', preparing 'scathing criticisms of Mabo and the Royal Commission into Aboriginal Deaths in Custody' (p. 31). At the end of his essay, he lists further supposed motives animating anti-Bringing them home 'campaigners', perhaps including me. It is true, for instance, that I am a former leftist, although far from thinking that 'truth is simply the opposite of what [I] once believed', my views on Aboriginal issues and on racial matters generally have changed little from the then left-wing ideas I held in the early 1970s. Given his references to my 'mean-spirited' criticisms (pp. 33, 42), he no doubt believes that I am also someone who has 'little capacity for empathy' (p. 102). It seems I have been remiss in not adopting his own approach, taking every opportunity to stress my unbounded compassion and rectitude. Unfortunately however, I would find this rather distasteful. It reminds me of Emerson's maxim, 'the louder he talked of his honor, the faster we counted our spoons'.

The situation regarding mining companies, the Institute of Public Affairs, and my other writings on Aboriginal issues is also rather different from what Manne pretends. For a start, if he really believes that taking money from the mining industry compromises both me and the IPA, he should explain why, as editor of Quadrant, he requested and received funding from some of the same mining companies who support us. He seems to be implying that while he is too pure to be tainted by his funding, those of us without his admirable qualities are far more vulnerable.

And although Manne has claimed that mining companies 'have a great deal to lose or gain regarding the thrust of Aboriginal policy' (The Age, 2 March 1998), he should spell out their interest in the 'stolen generations' issue. Does he really think that publicising the defects of Bringing them home can have any consequences for how courts will deal with heritage or native title cases? In fact, the industry is very keen to avoid the 'stolen generations' issue, given that in recent years all large mining companies operating in Australia have put considerable efforts into developing close relations with national and regional Aboriginal organisations. They have nothing to gain and much to lose from supporting those who question the 'Aboriginal industry' position on the issue.

My attacks on Bringing them home have not helped the IPA's fund raising, and they have not helped my anthropological consultancy. Just before Betraying the Victims was released, for instance, I had been asked to join an advisory committee of

WMC Ltd. A couple of weeks later the invitation was withdrawn on the extraordinary grounds that it should not have been made in the first place. While WMC denied that my involvement with the controversy about the 'stolen generations' had prompted the withdrawal, it certainly seemed a strange coincidence. I would probably be better off if I stopped commenting on controversial Aboriginal issues, because it seems to scare off clients. But just as some academics continue teaching although they could earn more elsewhere, I find satisfaction in what I do and believe that it is worth doing.

Even Manne's suggestion that I consistently seek to undermine judgements or reports 'conspicuously sympathetic to the Aborigines' is specious and revealing. He seems to be implying that something purporting to be sympathetic to Aborigines should be immune from criticism. But it is a commonplace of social science (and common sense) that noble intentions do not necessarily produce good outcomes, and the thrust of much of my writing on Aboriginal issues has been to warn that seemingly attractive approaches may prove counter-productive. My criticisms of the Deaths in Custody Royal Commission, for instance, were focused solely on its emphasis on 'institutional racism' as the major explanation for Aboriginal disadvantage, one which I believe only reinforces a corrosive and disempowering sense of victimhood. And my strongest criticisms of the *Mabo* decision have been that it gives Aborigines an inferior form of title which limits their freedom. This much, at least, Manne does know, because he once published an article presenting my arguments for this view ('Shame about Aborigines', *Quadrant*, May 1997).

People who are prone to believe in conspiracies are usually impervious to information which casts doubt on their fantasies. Nevertheless, given that Manne casts me as having struck 'the first serious blow' in a supposed Howard Government backed 'right-wing' campaign against the 'stolen generations' (p. 31), some important matters should be stated for the record.

To the best of my recollection, I have never discussed *Bringing them home* with any members of the present government. In 1997, a former Liberal back-bencher, Russell Broadbent, rang to ask my opinion of the report. When I said that it had dealt irresponsibly with a very serious issue, and that ideally, the government should commission another inquiry which would be carried out with the appropriate rigour and probity, he ended the conversation, and I never heard from him again. In fact, the individuals with whom I have had the most frequent and extensive discussions about the 'stolen generations' – and Aboriginal issues generally – are two former Labor ministers, Peter Walsh and Gary Johns. Walsh has been a particularly trenchant and longstanding public critic of *Bringing them home* and the 'stolen generations' inquiry, both as an *Australian Financial Review* columnist, and in his current position as a columnist for the *Adelaide Review*. Manne makes no mention of this, perhaps because it could muddy his picture of a Howard government-supported right-wing campaign.

Furthermore, as he no doubt remembers, it was Manne himself who informed me that the Government submission to the Senate Inquiry into the Stolen Generation had used my work, or as he wrote in an email on April 11 last year, that I was one of the submission's 'fathers'. I subsequently obtained the document, and learnt a number of very significant facts which I had not known before – including that *Bringing them home* had grossly misrepresented Max Kamien's crucial Bourke study, wrongly claiming it had shown that one in every three Aboriginal adults had been separated from their families in childhood. If the Government were really running a campaign in which I had a starring role, surely it would have kept me in the loop so that I did not have to rely on fortuitous disclosures from Manne for such important details. One might also imagine that I would be asked to look over a submission I had 'fathered'. We all know that the Howard Government is inept at handling cultural controversies, but this would be something else again.

One of Manne's favoured sayings comes from Solzhenitsyn – 'slander is a hummable tune'. Sadly, it is a tune that Manne himself is fond of. He states that I claim 'almost all' of 'the thousands of Aborigines' who believed themselves 'to have been taken from their parents unjustly... were in the grip of collective hysteria and suffering from "false memory syndrome"' (p. 73). I have never written anything that could remotely justify this statement. Nor would I. Indeed, it is refuted by what Manne says about me elsewhere: 'In *Betraying the Victims* Brunton accepted that very many Aboriginal children had been separated from their mothers and communities by force' (p. 31). My only references to the 'false memory syndrome' have been to point out that its existence should have made the inquiry take appropriate steps to check as many of the stories it presented as possible in order to head off inevitable questions about the veracity of these stories. Although Manne neglects to mention the fact, in his judgement in the Cubillo–Gunner case Justice O'Loughlin noted that both claimants were engaged, even if not deliberately, in 'exercises of reconstruction' (Cubillo v Commonwealth, FCA 1084, para 125). However, Manne does say that it is 'obvious to commonsense' that the memories of some individuals who appeared before the inquiry, 'like all childhood memories, were likely to have been simplified and even distorted with the passage of time' (p. 30). What he notes is just 'commonsense', but when I say something similar it is 'grotesque', which is the term he used in the edited extract from the essay published in the *Age* and *Sydney Morning Herald* (March 31).

There are other gross misrepresentations in the essay. Manne uses quotations 'creatively' to make it appear as though I made statements which not only were never made, but which are the virtual opposite of what I actually said. Thus he writes '... the implication behind Brunton's criticism [of *Bringing them home*], namely that a comparison between Aboriginal and non-Aboriginal child removal involves a comparison of "like with like"... is self-evidently absurd' (pp. 34–35). But I did not say that the removals were the same. Indeed, I specifically wrote that 'the existence in various jurisdictions of special legislation which diminished the rights of Aborigines and made it easier to remove Aboriginal children was clearly racially discriminatory, and cannot be defended'. The 'like with like' is ripped from a sentence in the same paragraph where I criticised the report for making comparisons between Aboriginal and non-Aboriginal removals based on very different kinds of evidence, drawing conclusions about the latter 'largely from inferences, unsupported opinions, and questionable generalisations', rather than from accounts of the actual experiences of non-Aboriginal children (*Betraying the Victims*, p. 9).

Manne resorts to a similar tactic to make another finding of 'absurdity' against my methodological criticisms of *Bringing them home*, pretending that one of my reasons for questioning whether it faithfully depicted *evidence* presented to the inquiry was a failure to include verbatim extracts from all Aboriginal witnesses (pp. 32, 70). Had this been the basis for my questioning, it certainly would have been foolish. But it was not. I criticised the report for failing to include vital *summary information* about those witnesses who were taken, such as official reasons for original removal, whether the child was later returned to his or her family, and so on; and for omitting important summary demographic information that would have allowed comparison with other data sources on removed children. The absence of such summary information raised legitimate doubts about the representativeness of witnesses appearing before the inquiry, as well as the cases selected for discussion in the report. To anticipate and head off possible objections that *Bringing them home* had focused on actual experiences rather than on cold statistical data, I also noted that the stories in the report had come from only a minority of witnesses appearing before the inquiry. My discussion of this issue appeared under a sub-heading '*Failure to provide necessary summary data relating to witnesses*' (BtV, pp. 8–9), which should have made things sufficiently clear to even the most tendentious reader.

Manne makes a further finding of 'self-evident absurdity' about my suggestion that the inquiry could have requested amendments to its terms of reference to allow it to make a proper assessment of the similarities and differences between Aboriginal and non-Aboriginal child removals. How could it have afforded such an investigation with only $2 million in funding? he asks (p. 34). But my suggestion would only be 'self-evidently absurd' to someone who conveniently overlooked three important facts, one of which even appeared elsewhere in his essay. Firstly, the inquiry asked for, and obtained, amended terms of reference from the Keating government so it could consider compensation for those affected by the child removal policies. Secondly, as Manne himself notes, it also asked the Howard Government for more money (p. 5). While this was unsuccessful, it is hardly fanciful to think that a request to the previous government would have failed, particularly if it was argued that expansion would enhance the overall credibility of the inquiry, as well as head off possible future requests for an inquiry into non-Aboriginal child removals. This leads to the final point – the Royal Commission into Aboriginal Deaths in Custody provided a precedent showing that a Labor Government would extend the terms and cost of an inquiry into a sensitive issue relating to Aboriginal concerns far beyond what was originally planned.

So keen is Manne to assert the supposed 'absurdity' of my criticisms, that he catches Bringing them home in friendly fire. He assures readers that it would have been impractical for the inquiry to have followed the kind of investigation I would urge, which would have involved testing the evidence of witnesses against documentary evidence about their cases (pp. 33–4). Unfortunately for him however, HREOC claimed that testing had been done. On its website it stated that the inquiry 'conducted extensive searches and analysis of historical documents and records which substantiated its findings'. In Betraying the Victims, where this was noted (p. 5), I pointed out that HREOC should have provided more information to support this claim, including the number of witness statements or submissions that were actually checked against the records. Furthermore, despite Manne's misleading attempt to suggest otherwise, I did not state that the highly intensive kind of investigation carried out by the Royal Commission was appropriate for the HREOC inquiry. In Betraying the Victims I said that the cases considered by the Royal Commission indicated a more complex picture of removals than the one presented by Bringing them home, and this was the major point of my comparison. I also noted that the Royal Commission showed it was possible to obtain information about the reasons for removal from various sources (pp. 7–9).

Manne states that my treatment of the genocide issue, which occupies a substantial portion of Betraying the Victims, is 'unsatisfactory', and that 'several of my criticisms' are 'little more than point scoring'. He says that both Bringing them home and I have failed to distinguish between the pre-WWII policy of biological absorption and the post-war policy of socio-cultural assimilation. As the sole example of my supposed point-scoring he offers my reference to the famous *Aborigines Claim Citizen Rights* manifesto for the 1938 Sesquicentennial Australia Day protest, written by Aboriginal activists Jack Patten and William Ferguson, which included a passage advocating cultural and biological absorption. Not only does Manne think this largely irrelevant to the question of the relationship between child removals and genocide, he also suggests that the passage may have been included at the prompting of the fascist literary critic 'Inky' Stephenson, who was then assisting Patten and Ferguson (pp. 35–7, 41).

A number of issues need to be unpacked here. In *Betraying the Victims* I dealt with the arguments actually presented in *Bringing them home*, not those that Manne might have wished it to make. The report clearly stated that the child removals were 'genocidal' because they were instigated to achieve the objective of assimilation (see BtV, p.10). Consequently, an examination of the attitudes prominent Aboriginal campaigners once held towards assimilation was appropriate and necessary. Furthermore, whereas Manne now only seems willing to argue that some senior pre-WWII administrators, in talking about 'breeding out the colour', were guilty of 'genocidal thoughts' (pp. 39–40), *Bringing them home* was not talking about 'thoughts'. It was saying that actual *practices* were genocidal, and that the term might even be applicable to practices that persisted into the 1980s (BTH, p. 274). A number of matters were relevant for an assessment of *Bringing them home*'s arguments. These included its gross misrepresentation of a document relating to mixed motives that was crucial for its 'genocide' finding, because it was the matter of motives that had earlier caused the Royal Commission into Aboriginal Deaths in Custody to reject a similar charge (see *National Report*, vol. 5, pp. 28–35; BtV, pp. 11–12). I considered these matters under eight different headings, although no-one relying on Manne's account of my paper would ever realise this.

At first glance, Manne's suggestion that Stephenson was behind the apparent support for absorption sounds plausible. However, in March 1998, after he raised the possibility in a newspaper column, I sent him evidence taken from Jack Horner's biography of Ferguson, Vote Ferguson for Aboriginal Freedom, and Andrew Marcus's book, Governing Savages, refuting his suggestion. As I pointed out, 'one of the reasons behind Ferguson's split with Patten later in 1938 was Ferguson's suspicion of Stephenson and his motives. Yet, as Marcus makes clear, a year and a half after this split, Ferguson was still advocating "the gradual absorption of the aborigines into the white race"'. The fact that Manne simply repeats his suggestion without referring to or addressing this seemingly fatal contrary evidence does not enhance confidence in his intellectual integrity.

Manne also accuses me of being unable 'to understand, let alone answer, the arguments developed since 1997 by Raimond Gaita' and himself. He attacks my 'humourless' article on the 'unconceived generations' published in *Quadrant* in May 1998, claiming it is based on a failure to see the 'difference between prescribing the pill and forcibly removing children with the purpose of making a people disappear' (p. 41). In fact, this partly tongue-in-cheek piece was written to show where a combination of Manne and Gaita's position and *Bringing them home's* kind of arguments might lead. But it was probably unwise to write in a less than deadly earnest manner, because I should have heeded McKenzie Wark's observation that both Manne and Gaita have 'a cloth ear for irony'. Nevertheless, the article did make a very serious point.

I specifically accepted that genocide involves the idea that certain people have the 'right to determine who should and who should not inhabit the world', as Gaita puts it. But the same logic that *Bringing them home* had used to show that the child removals contravened Article II (e) of the Genocide Convention could also be used to show that family planning programs contravened Article II (d), which precludes 'imposing measures intended to prevent births within the group'. In fact, this has long been argued by some radical Black Americans and Aborigines.

Although I personally believe that giving advice on birth control to anyone desiring it is proper, some Third World family planning programs have not just innocently 'prescribed the pill' to tribal and peasant women. There is a fair amount of evidence indicating that at different times and places 'duress' and 'undue influence' (to adopt terms from *Bringing them home*) have been used to sterilise women without their informed consent, or to provide them with dangerous forms of contraception. Furthermore, some of the most vocal proponents of the post-WWII 'population explosion' panic came out of the eugenics movement which Manne so strongly – and justifiably – condemns. Prominent advocates, such as William Vogt, made remarks that betray 'genocidal thoughts' and 'racist contempt' (to use Gaita's words) every bit as callous as those that Manne has found in A.O. Neville's reported comments about eventually forgetting that there were ever any Aborigines in Australia (p. 40).

Vogt, for instance, wrote in 1948 that 'the greatest tragedy that China could suffer at the present time would be a reduction in her death rate' (my IPA Backgrounder, *The End of the Overpopulation Crisis?*, December 1998, discusses these matters in more detail and provides references). In other words, while Neville did not necessarily wish to see a single premature death, Vogt was calling for it on a mass scale. So if Manne or Gaita (or *Bringing them home*) say we must take seriously the argument that those who spoke of 'breeding out the colour' were urging 'genocide', we must also consider whether Australia's support for Third World birth control programs may, at the very least, constitute 'complicity in genocide' (a crime under Article III of the Genocide Convention). It is Manne who is unwilling to contemplate this possibility. Indeed, when I raised it during our debate on ABC's 7.30 *Report* on March 31, he adopted a tone which was – to borrow his phrase – 'sneering and contemptuous'.

Manne's failure to comprehend his own arguments goes further, however. During an email exchange in April 2000, I said that if he thought Neville expressed 'genocidal thoughts' in his reported comments, he should also acknowledge that Aboriginal tribal elders who pressured women to kill 'half-caste' babies – something which occurred in at least some places in early stages of contact with Europeans (see *BtV*, p. 13) – were guilty of 'genocidal deeds'. After all, they held the belief that certain kinds of people, whom they perceived as being quite distinct from themselves, should not inhabit the world.

Manne's response was most revealing. He said that I did not understand his arguments, because to him, genocide was the desire 'to remove a distinct people from the face of the earth'. This seemed just what I was saying. But he then added that genocide 'is the kind of thing that intellectuals dream about not tribal elders'. This extraordinary statement combines an impossible omniscience about what tribal elders may or may not 'dream about', with a considerable ignorance about actual tribal behaviour (see e.g. Lawrence Keeley's *War Before Civilization*). Even more bizarre, Manne went on to claim that it was not just any old intellectuals who had these dreams, but those with a 19th century world view. Indeed, the fact that I had challenged him to condemn tribal elders for adopting what was a modern European view point was evidence that I did not understand the sort of argument he was making. I stand convicted. I am unable 'to understand, let alone answer' this kind of logic.

The above comments cover only some of the defects I have identified in the dozen or so pages of *In Denial* that refer to me. The others can be found in the rebuttal on the IPA website. However, I think I have done enough here to raise grave doubts about Manne's judgement and his approach to factual evidence. Given that the great majority of their readers will not follow them into the archives, one of the essential requirements for good historians is the ability to present reliable accounts of the documents they examine. *In Denial* shows that Manne lacks this ability. Eventually, we may obtain a 'better history' of the Aboriginal child removals, but it is most unlikely that it could ever come from Robert Manne.

Ron Brunton

by Inga Clendinnen

First published in the *Australian's Review Of Books*, 9 May 2001.

April's *Australian Review Of Books* offered an array of perspectives of our past: on history in Australia (Stephen Matchett); race relations in Australian history (Keith Windschuttle, Glen McLaren, Alan Atkinson, Jack Egan); race relations as represented in a famous piece of Australian historical fiction (Garry Kinnane); and a Shandyesque slice of fictionalised history, including, we are promised, 'psychotic episodes', by the astonishing Cannibal Jack Diaper (Nicolas Rothwell). Who says history is dead? If some of the questions raised for discussion were close to vexatious, that is the way of it with lively issues. (Examples: If a body of whites armed with rifles are in control of the high ground and a body of Aboriginal warriors are up to their chins in a river, *but still in possession of their spears*, is what happens next a battle, or a turkey shoot? How many murders make a massacre? If the Native Police in Victoria in the first part of the 19th century didn't kill anybody, does that mean that the Native Police in Queensland in the latter part of the century didn't kill anybody either? And so on.)

Meanwhile, Egan's letter reminds us that some very old questions are still not answered. As editor of the collection *Buried Alive*, Egan knows the early colonial documentation well, and he takes Henry Reynolds to task for too swift a judgment on one famous episode: the gruesome orders issued by governor Phillip to a punitive expedition sent out after the ambush-spearing of his convict gamekeeper John McEntire in mid November, 1790. The colony's surgeons predicted that McEntire would die from his wound, which he duly did, there was no known provocation, the offence was wilful murder by persons unknown. In response, Phillip instructed his troops to capture any two male Aborigines found in the Botany Bay area, the probable culprit's home territory, and to kill 10 more. The heads of those slain were to be cut off, put in the bags provided and brought back to the settlement, presumably for public display.

Gruesome indeed. The premonitory shadow of Kurtz seems to fall over the Australian scrub.

Reynolds invokes the orders to help substantiate his claim that 'practically all early governors advocated the use of terror to crush Aboriginal resistance', and quotes Phillip's own statement that he was 'determined to strike a decisive blow, in order at once to convince [the Aborigines] of our superiority, and to infuse a universal terror'. Reynolds concludes with a challenge: How can arbitrary terror be consistent with Christian conscience and a high value placed on morality and law?

Egan questions Reynolds's reading by reminding us that the expedition was a total failure, to no one's particular surprise, and that Phillip's overall record was good. So how to explain those scandalous orders? As a historian I have an abiding admiration for Reynolds, who in difficult territory somehow stays close to the ground and typically avoids simplification. On this particular issue, however, I think he nods.

If we look closely, we notice several odd things about that infamous expedition. First, the formally authorised violence was hedged about by a bristle of restrictions. The orders made clear that only soldiers were permitted to fire on any native, and then only if directly ordered to do so, or in self-defence. Phillip had no intention of tolerating, much less encouraging, white vigilantism. The troops were also instructed that at all times the specific reason for the punitive action had to be made clear, which, given the state of verbal communication at this early stage of contact, was a tall order. He also reminded everyone within earshot that all native property, often pilfered by convicts and soldiers alike for sale in the market for artifacts back in Britain, was sacrosanct, and enjoyed the full protection of British law.

The expedition was also out of character. Phillip had borne his own spearing three months before with fortitude and admirable anthropological 'cool', diagnosing the sudden aggression as no more than an individual expression of panic. (I think he was wrong there.) While he had not the least doubt that he and his compatriots were the legitimate new lords of the soil, he had gambled a great deal of time, patience and personal suffering to bring about friendship with the local tribe. He had long been anxious to persuade its members to come into the settlement, to live under British law and to absorb the benefits of British civilisation. Indeed, he had tried to effect this outcome by twice resorting to forcible kidnappings in the hope of finding a reliable go-between. (Against the odds, it worked: he bagged the wily 'Bennelong', as we call him.) He had also hoped such a rapprochement would put an end to the Aborigines' apparently casual spearings of convicts in the 'woods'. Seventeen British, nearly all of them unarmed, had been speared since first contact, some of them fatally, yet to that point Phillip had steadfastly refused to retaliate, insisting that the native attacks were provoked by convict misconduct.

With the McEntire spearing he knew the gamble had failed. A friendly accommodation had been reached with the local natives only a handful of weeks before when they had 'come in' to Sydney Town, in baffling response to his own spearing, yet the new friendship had not put an end to Aboriginal violence. And this attack was notably more sinister than those before it, being a planned, murderous assault, and its target an armed man. (The British needed to believe that all Aborigines were terrified of muskets.)

Furthermore, in Phillip's thinking McEntire had a perfect right to be where he was, innocently hunting game in the open larder of the bush. Phillip's Aboriginal friends had readily named the spearman, they had made soothing noises about bringing him in – and had shown not the least inclination to do so. Justice had to be done, and the Aborigines had to be brought to respect the rule of law. What to do next? What he did was order out the expedition – and select Watkin Tench to lead it.

Tench was famously sympathetic to Aborigines. Phillip also condescended to ask Tench's advice regarding the reprisals. As we would expect, Tench softened the terms, urging that the British should content themselves with capturing six men, some of whom would suffer exemplary capital punishment while others could be released when their lesson in British justice was well-learnt. Phillip refined Tench's suggestions further: if the new tally of six men could not be captured, six men were to be shot. If six were captured, he would hang two and send the rest to Norfolk Island. The sum was straightforward: if Tench used muskets six men might die; if he refrained from using muskets – if the focus was on capture, not killing – only two. Phillip knew Tench would be loathe to shoot. In the event, the 'terrific procession' of 52 men which came stumbling back after three days slogging through hard country and December heat brought not a single captive with them. They had sighted some fleeing natives, they had chatted with their friend Colbee who, despite Phillip's efforts to dissuade him, had followed them to see the fun, and that was the total of their success. So what did Phillip do next? He sent out a smaller but still formidable expedition of 39 men on the same mission. This time they were to march at night, as Tench says with a carefully straight face, 'both for the sake of secrecy and to avoid the heat of the day'. This time they saw not a single native. Their main excitement was when several men, including Tench, came perilously close to drowning as they floundered in a patch of quicksand.

When I first read this, I kept expecting Colbee and some grinning companions to step from behind the trees to rescue them. The British might have seen no natives, but the natives had surely seen them.

Tench's attitude to these excursions was, throughout, one of irony. He knew that a mob of British soldiers crashing through the bush had minimal chance of sighting, much less seizing Aboriginal men on their home ground. Phillip must have known that too. He also must have borne some local ridicule, especially after the second weary, muddy expedition came straggling in. So what was he up to? I am exploring the fine detail of that elsewhere, but for the moment I suggest that he was no more hopeful than Tench of achieving his claimed objectives and that his primary concern was to stage a histrionic performance of the terror of British law in accordance with the fine late-18th-century tradition of formal floggings, elaborate death rites, and breathless last-minute reprieves and repentances.

I think the performance was designed to impress both the (increasingly restless) convicts and soldiers within the settlement, and the watching Aborigines inside and around it. In sum, my view is that Phillip sent out the troops, and then sent them out again, to remind British settlers and convicts that violence towards Aborigines was the monopoly of the soldiery and the prerogative of the state, while the tribes were given the opportunity to reflect on the tolerant Phillip's capacity for organised violence if he were tried too far. He threatened them with collective punishment, in defiance of British protocols, not because he had a taste for racist terror but because he had a good anthropological eye. What the tribes cared about was their fighting strength, individual injuries being simply shrugged off. Phillip knew that if he could not teach the tribesmen to refrain from all violence against whites, he would not be able to protect them, and the wolves would be loosed upon them.

Racist terror came soon enough. Three years after his departure, Phillip's ream of a unitary commonwealth of whites and blacks living peaceably under British law was dead. The war over the land had been declared. While some Aborigines lived reduced lives within the white colony, endemic violence flared along the boundary between the two societies, and 'wild' Aborigines plundered the new settlers along the Hawkesbury and around Parramatta.

Settlers' huts were burnt almost as fast as they were built. In May 1795, whole families of natives were thought to be assembling near the Hawkesbury to raid the ripening corn on which the colony depended. (They probably were; the onset of winter was always a hard time.) The indefatigable chronicler, judge-attorney David Collins tells us what happened next:

> Captain Paterson directed a party of the [NSW] corps to be sent from Parramatta, with instructions to destroy as many they could meet with of the wood tribe and, in the hope of striking terror, to erect gibbets in different places, whereon the bodies of all those they might kill were to be hung.

In the event, no bodies were strung up although Collins tells us that several natives were reported killed, and some prisoners – 'a cripple, five women and some children' – were taken and sent to Sydney. In February 1796, the governor issued further regulations.

While it remained forbidden to fire at natives 'wantonly', settlers were issued muskets and ordered to come to each others' aid when there was threat of attack. There was nothing histrionic about this violence. Vigilantism was now licensed, indeed declared a matter of obligation; black bodies would hang from the trees. In those few years we had come a long way from Phillip's solemn pedagogical miming of the awful power of British law.

Is it worth fussing over a single individual's intentions when outcomes seem unaffected? I am persuaded it is, for two main reasons: we owe a moral duty of justice to our fellow humans, including the dead ones, and social analysts need to beware easy ascriptions of simple intentions if their disciplines are to retain their social utility. We need to remember, with Ivan Turgenev, that the heart of another is a dark forest, to be penetrated with alertness and steady curiosity. Of course, my analysis of Phillip's motives runs counter to Phillip's own crisp statement cited by Reynolds. But Phillip was a loner; a man unlikely to confide his deepest strategies. The intricacies of his intentions can be better retrieved from a close reading of his actions through time and changing contexts, mod-ified by his own changing access to information, than from fragments from particular public texts. I don't know how Christian Phillip was, but he was not a racist in any sense I understand. If I had to categorise him, always an unsatis-factory business with humans, I would call him an idealist of a flexible kind, being ready to modify strategies to achieve those ideals as new information came in.

While he recognised that Aborigines were certainly different from the British, he never doubted their common humanity. That confidence led him to believe that these 'shivering savages' would find comfort and security under the

British umbrella, and in time would flourish there – if they could be persuaded to try the experiment. Not a racist, then, nor an assimilationist – he neither expected nor desired complete Aboriginal integration – but perhaps Australia's first multiculturalist.

The tension between intention and outcome has come to dominate recent debate over *Bringing them home*, the report into the separation of part-Aboriginal and Torres Strait Islander children from their families, which was presented to Federal Parliament in May 1997, and now commonly known as the 'Stolen Generations' report. Given their lack of time, money and resources, the authors decided on a primary strategy of retelling some of the stories they had been listening to. As we would expect, the stories were impressionistic. They could not pretend to complete factual accuracy, much less to sustained legal relevance. Terrified children remember their own nightmare experiences, not the complicated actuality around them, and these particular children could not test their recollections against those of trusted adults because they had been taken from them. Nonetheless, the impact was powerful and the early response sympathetic. It was generally agreed that the authors had performed their central task well: they had brought the Government and the Australian people to awareness of a great wrong perpetrated against generations of Aboriginal families. Over the years the most manifest opinion seems to have changed, with increasingly bitter debate over the report's methodology, its conceptual frame, its findings, its recommendations and its motives.

The battles have been fought on the small battlefields of literary and academic journals, and by self-selected champions in the opinion and letters pages of leading newspapers. The general population has remained by and large silent, although my guess is that it was the moral energies released by the report which fuelled the surge of middle-class Australians towards 'reconciliation', and set hundreds of people meeting and thousands of people marching at the end of 2000, with high hopes for the new millennium.

When I first read the Human Rights Commission report some months after its publication, I already knew something of its contents. I was nonetheless unprepared for its impact on me: for the power over my imagination exercised by the stories; and by the implications of their terrible cumulative meanings. I felt at once betrayed, ashamed, chagrined and, above all, stupid: much of what was done had been done in my lifetime, so how could I have let myself remain ignorant of it? I also felt helpless: how could such injuries ever be healed? I suspect that many Australians who had previously given little thought to race relations responded much as I did.

I was helped out of this unprofitable morass by Robert Manne's essay on the stolen generations, first delivered as a lecture in November 1997, six months after the release of the Human Rights and Equal Opportunities Commission report, and reprinted in Manne's *The Way We Live Now* (Text Publishing, 1998.) The essay was written in Manne's characteristic window-pane prose and moral and intellectual lucidity. Given the complexities of the issues and the fragile nature of the written evidence, he was properly cautious, asking his readers 'to regard everything I say as tentative and provisional'. He made some criticisms of the report, as in its estimate of the percentage of children taken. He also draws a subtle and essential distinction between the mere proclamation of good intentions, and our own critical evaluation of the subsequent actions: the old 'words-versus-actions' issue.

He judges the 'social welfarist-good intentions defence' of government policies to be in bad faith: 'it is absolutely false to claim that the motives of those who made or executed the social policy were of a social-welfare kind. They were driven by altogether different motives.' Their core motive, in his view, was to keep Australia white. The distinction blurs slightly when he allows that while 'the policy makers and agents of the state viewed these [Aboriginal] children and the worlds from which they had come through racist spectacles they genuinely believed that in taking the children from their family and culture ... they were acting in the best interests of the child.' Why, then, is the 'social-welfarist defence' vacuous? Blanket ascriptions of motives to whole categories of people make me nervous.

Manne also retraced the hard intellectual route he had followed to arrive at the acceptance of the word 'genocide' as descriptive of some phases and aspects of Australia's Aboriginal policies. He remained unsure as to whether the commission had made the legal case for such an application, but he had decided, after reflecting on Raimond Gaita's 'sterilisation' example – (a thought experiment which invites us to think of the 'forcible sterilisation' of a people aimed at their extinction) – that genocide could be effected without resort to murderous means. On murderous intentions, he wavers. He allows that 'violence against Aborigines was only not used but was generally unthinkable to those who designed child-removal policies', and that even in the Western Australia and the Northern Territory of the 1930s, the administrators who (briefly) implemented policies designed to effect the ultimate 'elimination' of people of mixed descent were not driven by race hatred, but by the conviction that 'the elimination of 'half-castes' would constitute an unambiguous good' – for, presumably, racist reasons.

But while he is no assimilationist, he grants (against the report's arguments) that 'socio-cultural assimilation does not seem to me to be describable as genocidal', and that the charge of genocide for the whole period 'remains contentious between people of good will'.

In his recent essay 'In Denial', the first publication of The Quarterly Essay (Black Inc, 2001), Manne still acknowledges the report's defects, but his attitude to the critics of the report has hardened, because he believes that a concerted right-wing conspiracy centred on the literary journal Quadrant exists, with tentacles reaching out to embrace leading members of the conservative Government and some of the bigger players in mining and other ventures, and that this conspiracy has mounted a 'serious and effective campaign' against the Bringing them home report, its authors, its supporters and its emotional and political impact. And now he is ready to say that in the pre-1940 period in Australia 'thinking of a genocidal kind' occasionally emerged, most noticeably in the 1937 conference of Aboriginal administrators, when 'genocidal thought and administrative practice touched'.

Manne also states that all the people who have clustered around Quadrant in the last three years have moved from 'the promise of "genuine debate" on Aboriginal policy to the reality of atrocity denialism in the David Irving mode'. In his even more recent review of Paul Kelly's book, 100 Years: The Australian Story, in the April issue of the Australian Book Review, in the course of chiding Kelly for moral shallowness, Manne makes clear that he is now convinced that the policy of Aboriginal child removal drew its strength from racism for its whole duration, and that during the 'biological geneticism' period of the '30s it was genocidal as well. And because these conclusions have become so clear to him, he now judges those who reject them to be wilfully blind and thus intellectually and morally corrupt. The report's charge of genocide has been revivified, and Orwell has transformed into Blake.

There are certainly more than a couple of rascals in the anti-report line-up, but what I hear most clearly as I reread their articles and letters – a task made easy by Manne's impeccable chronicling of materials – is a simpler thing: outrage at the use of that word 'genocide', accompanied by the slamming-shut of minds. As an academic I sympathise with the analyst's eagerness to assay such key terms: to trace their judicial and moral genealogy; to see how far they can be stretched without tearing.

Nonetheless, I remain persuaded that the persistent invocation of the term 'genocide' by the authors of the report and their later supporters to describe any phase of Australian policies to Aborigines was not only ill-judged, but a moral, intellectual and (as it is turning out) a political disaster. I am reasonably sophisticated in various modes of intellectual discussion, but when I see the word 'genocide' I still see Gypsies and Jews being herded into trains, into pits, into ravines, and behind them the shadowy figures of Armenian women and children being marched into the desert by armed men. I see deliberate mass murder: innocent people identified by their killers as a distinctive entity being done to death by organised authority. I believe that to take the murder out of genocide is to render it vacuous, and I believe with Orwell that it is essential to keep such words mirror-bright because, given the nature of human affairs, we will surely continue to need them. As for morality: in the task of reconstructing intentions (as in the earlier discussion of governor Phillip), motives must be distinguished from outcomes, and hunted down not only in words but in the details of actions in their varying contexts. They will not submit easily to labelling.

As for the political effects: I think the report's use of the word 'genocide' was a political disaster because I don't know what was gained by it, and a great deal was certainly lost. At least some of the resistance to its shaking stories and their seriously uncomfortable moral and political implications was facilitated by anger at that charge being levelled promiscuously against individuals who perhaps were less informed or less imaginative than they might have been, but who in many cases acted in good faith.

I have just been watching the video of the Good Friday, 1997 edition of ABC TV's *Compass* made immediately before the release of the report. In the course of the program, a man named Bernie Clark was interviewed. He had gone to Darwin as a Uniting Church social worker in 1965 to help the older children from the recently closed Croker Island Mission to find jobs, and he had just submitted a report to the Human Rights Commission to explain how it was back then. In 1965 he had come in at the tail end of the more vigorous experiments in assimilation, and he had come to regret them profoundly. Nonetheless, and with fine honesty, he acknowledged that had he been an administrator in the '60s he would have done the same thing. He said: 'We wanted to help people to maximise their opportunities in life. Now I realise we were destroying their capacity to maximise their opportunities of life.'

Intentions matter. So, of course, do outcomes, but the connections are not always evident.

The vulnerability of children, combined with their apparent malleability, rouses powerful emotions in most of us, not all of them conscious, especially when we see the children as belonging to 'us'. Social and moral catastrophes litter the history of child welfare. Consider the experience of the young Gitta Sereny, working for the United Nations Relief and Rehabilitation

Administration in the US sector of Germany in 1946 as a child-welfare investigative officer. The main task of these officers was to rescue 'unaccompanied children', whether displaced or orphaned or abandoned, from the streets and the camps.

There was another group, too: children selected by the Nazis in defeated Poland for their Aryan physical characteristics, taken from their parents, transported to Germany, and after a period of observation and testing for physical and social acceptability were adopted out to 'worthy' German families, which meant good Nazi supporters. The adopting families were told the children were German orphans recovered from the regained Eastern territories. The Nazis' intention was to improve the war-depleted race with these 'racially valuable' children, who were, of course, destined to lose all contact and memory of their Polish kin. Perhaps 200,000 Polish children were abducted to Germany.

Sereny became involved in tracking down such children, taking them from their German families and returning them to their Polish ones. She gives an account of one such intervention in the magazine *Talk* for November, 1999. (I am indebted to Helen Garner for sending me Sereny's article.) It is a painful story. The children, a boy and a girl, both about six, had been living with their Bavarian family for three years when Sereny arrived at the door. They were – transparently – happy, healthy and well-loved. The mother, intuiting why this official had visited them, was especially eager to demonstrate how well they were cared for: 'You know now, don't you, Fraulein, that they are ours? That they were given to us?'

Sereny did her duty. Persuading the mother to give her a Christmas photograph of the children taken soon after their arrival (the mother thought she wanted it because they were so pretty) they were identified as twins taken from a Polish couple living near Lodz. Meanwhile, Sereny had moved on. She had to 'take' only one child, a little boy, herself. She still remembers 'the inconsolable grief of the couple who loved the five-year-old and the wild anger of the child, who had no memory of his birth parents or native language, and for whom his German parents were the world'. Sereny acknowledged that in all her experience in this period, she 'never handled or heard of a single case in which the German foster or adoptive parents had treated the kidnapped child with anything but love'.

Some months later she accidentally met the pretty twins from Bavaria, Johann and Marie, in a holding centre where they were meant to be learning Polish before their repatriation. The once-lively Marie 'was scrunched up in a chair, her eyes closed, the lids transparent, her thumb in her mouth'.

At six she was wetting her bed and taking food only from a bottle. But Johann responded. He rushed at Sereny, striking her with fists and feet, shouting

'Du! Du! Du!' Three days later the children left for Poland. About 25,000 Polish children of the 200,000 reported taken were retrieved and sent home.

Good intentions do not mean injury is always avoided, and not all injuries arise from bad intentions. Deciphering human motives, including one's own, is a complicated business, and tracing outcomes even more so, but morality is made intelligent only by evaluating human intentions, and by tracing those intentions' actual outcomes. Sereny again: 'I have not solved the question of what was the best solution for these children – and I don't think that anyone can.'

Politically, I am on Manne's side, but I don't like adversarial history, and I don't like adversarial politics either. (When did you last change your mind because you lost an argument?) There has always been an impulse among certain kinds of politicians to reduce complicated matters to slogans in a familiar expression of contempt for the intelligence of ordinary people. In intellectuals the characteristic flaw is moralism, which discourages both subtlety in analysis, and patience and generosity in judgment. Along with a lot of other Australians, I am committed to a decent reconciliation between the indigenous population and the rest of us: to the recognition of the injuries they have suffered generation by generation, and to amelioration of the consequences of those injuries. Human dignity, both theirs and ours, demands it. Those ends can be achieved only by decisions arising from the informed understanding of seriously complicated issues by a substantial majority of the Australian people.

I have a tough politician friend who said of another friend, also in politics, 'Well – his heart's in the right place, but he can't count.' In a democracy it is necessary to be able to count.

Inga Clendinnen

CORRESPONDENCE

from Michael Duffy

Robert Manne's claim that criticisms of parts of the *Bringing them home* report represent an 'attempt to deny ... that a really terrible injustice occurred' is wrong. Anyone who has read my columns in the *Courier Mail* or *Daily Telegraph* will be aware how he has misrepresented them to reach such an insulting conclusion. I don't know why he bothered: there is an enormous gulf between us even when my views are described accurately.

I incline towards scepticism when considering stories of the oppression of Aboriginal people in the past, whereas Manne has a tendency to exaggerate. I accept that my approach risks minimising or overlooking cruelty and can be easily parodied as heartless or racist. But maybe more attention needs to be paid to the potentially harmful effects of the approach Manne favours. I refer in particular to its influence on the selection of policies to redress Aboriginal suffering.

The deeper question underlying much debate over many Aboriginal issues is the old question regarding assimilation. This is not an absolute question but a relative one: should there be more or less of it, and in which circumstances? Of course this is hugely complicated, and all Aboriginal people experience different degrees of assimilation in different areas of their lives. This deep question rarely surfaces, because assimilation has such a bad historical reputation (often violent, racist, patronising) that few people dare argue for it openly today. But assimilation as a desirable possibility in some circumstances, to be encouraged by government policy, is emerging into the open again, although usually under different names, such as self-modernisation.

Arguments about history affect people's attitudes to assimilation and vice versa. People in favour of policies promoting integration look for support in examples of successful assimilation in the past. And other people, who feel that Aboriginal history is an almost unrelieved record of oppression and misery, feel that this lends support to modern policies favouring independent development for Aboriginal people.

I know little of Robert Manne's views on contemporary Aboriginal policies, but most of the people I know who are influenced by his view of history are supporters of the communal land rights/traditional culture/permanent welfare paradigm of the past few decades. I believe this has been a disaster for many Aboriginal people, and that views such as those expressed in the Bringing them home report (e.g. on genocide) are an emotional roadblock hindering the consideration of alternative policies.

I would argue that the view of history often taken in Bringing them home is exaggerated and encourages the adoption of modern policies more for their symbolic value than their outcomes. The main example of this sort of thing is that a thousand times more ink has been expended in the Australian press in the past six years in arguing for John Howard to apologise to 'the stolen generations' than for something to be done to provide the Aboriginal people in remote communities with jobs.

Of course, no one is going to admit they don't care about such jobs – it just so happens that, after 30 years of considerable public debate and government expenditure and action, they don't exist.

I realise that many readers will disagree with the above argument. However, it's one I've put consistently over the past few years, and is a long way from the parody of my views presented by Manne.

Michael Duffy

CORRESPONDENCE

from Rod Moran

May I respond to Robert Manne's comments in the first issue of the *Australian Quarterly Essay* concerning my book *Massacre Myth*?

The volume is an unprecedented detailed forensic and documentary examination of the 1927 Royal Commission into allegations of mass murder of Aborigines in the hinterland of Forrest River Mission in WA's Kimberley region.

Neither journalists nor historians have previously accessed some of the material on which I drew in my many years of research. Further, the proceedings of the Royal Commission, which found against the police, have never been subjected to the close disassembly that I have undertaken to test the veracity of its findings.

On the basis of those findings, two policemen were arrested, charged with murder, refused bail and held over for committal proceedings. In the event, when the evidence was tested in Court before Magistrate Kidson, it was found that the Prosecution, led by Albert (later Sir Albert) Wolff, failed to establish even a *prima facie* case that a single Aborigine had been murdered, let alone the 11 the Royal Commissioner alleged.

Indeed, as anyone acquainted with the Royal Commission knows, during its proceedings Commissioner Wood himself admitted on record that no evidence had been adduced that would justify a verdict of murder by a jury. Yet, he went on to make just such a finding.

Ultimately, the two officers were discharged with no case to answer. In the succeeding decades no substantive evidence ever emerged that could have reactivated the charges against the police.

With respect, I have to say I find Professor Manne's approach in this matter astonishing. He cites the Royal Commission, Dr Neville Green's book *The Forrest River Massacres* and the stories told by Aborigines of the region as the indisputable evidence that foul mass murder had occurred at Forrest River.

This is a paradigm example of one of the most fundamental logical fallacies – the argument from authority. How an academic in Professor Manne's position could take such an approach is perplexing, given the gravity of the allegations involved.

The suppressed assumptions in Professor Manne's comments are clear. They are: that the Commissioner's findings were cogent and supported by the testimony, that Dr Green's efforts in this matter are reliable and that the stories told by some Aborigines about the supposed events of 1926 are true.

Unlike Professor Manne, I have investigated all three assumptions in considerable detail over many years and found them to be incorrect. If he has read my book, and with an open mind, I believe he would know this was the case.

Further, at page 184 of *Massacre Myth* I analyse out what is probably the grain of truth in the whole affair. It was entirely missed by the Commissioner, as was so much else. I will leave your readers to follow this matter up themselves in my book.

Professor Manne also says it is unlikely that evidence and logic in the matter will establish my case as the more plausible account of the Forrest River affair. In this regard, it was heartening to see that Dr David Day, an internationally esteemed Australian historian, has rewritten his comments on the Forrest River allegations in the recently issued second edition of his award-winning *Claiming a Continent: A New History of Australia*. This revision was made after he had read my book.

Moreover, *Massacre Myth* was launched by Professor Geoffrey Bolton, now pro-Chancellor of Murdoch University, and one of the nation's most senior historians. It contains a Foreword by Sir Francis Burt, former Chief Justice of WA, described by his peers in recent years as the finest legal mind of his generation.

In 1994 Sir Francis commented in private correspondence in the following manner:

> I have some book knowledge of the 'Onmalmeri massacre' – so called – the subject of the royal commission conducted by Magistrate Wood in 1927. It was, for many reasons, for which Wood was not entirely responsible, a very unsatisfactory inquiry. It would seem to have been the case that no finding or fact, which could be accepted with any confidence, was made and this, sad to say, has created a situation in which imagination can run unrestrained to present a picture to the young under the guise of historical truth and that...does nothing to promote reconciliation between black and white Australians.

I don't offer this information by way of an argument from authority. I believe the complete unreliability of Reverend Gribble, chief accuser in the case, is established through my analysis of the Royal Commission and the Court proceedings, in tandem with an investigation of other documentary evidence and the oral histories of the affair.

All of this is entirely independent of the views of those cited above.

I mention them to indicate that minds other than mine, individuals with substantive qualifications in the weighing of evidence, have carefully examined what I have written and agree a serious argument has been made in the matter concerning the accepted 'wisdom' in the case.

Professor Manne also says that, in the unlikely event I am considered right, Keith Windschuttle must surely understand that the refutation of the Forrest River allegations tells us nothing about killings on the frontier in WA and other regions of Australia between 1830 and the 1920s.

I am completely puzzled by this. I do not know of anywhere in his commentary that he makes such an absurd inference.

My suggestion is that the Forrest River allegations are myths. Their origin is to be found in the obsessions and background of a deeply disturbed man, the chief accuser, Reverend Ernest Gribble. No substantive evidence has ever emerged as to their truth, though the police, the Church, Government and Courts of the day, subjected them to wide investigation.

As to the reliability of the Court outcome, Sir Francis has commented in private correspondence in the following terms:

> I think it is worth pointing out, as I think it to be the fact, that Kidson was a very experienced magistrate and for that reason may well have chosen to hear the complaint and the Crown case was conducted by Albert Wolff who was without doubt a very competent prosecutor so that if the facts led in evidence [were] capable of making out the case Wolff would have made sure they did so. And if he had been of the opinion that Kidson had made a mistake and that in truth a prima facie case had been made out I have no doubt but that he would have seen to it that the Attorney-General presented an ex officio indictment. In other words reading between the lines it would seem to be fair to suppose that Wolff was not of the opinion that Kidson was wrong.

Further, for those who have not read the 1927 Royal Commission, the basis for the charges of wilful murder against the police, the following are only some aspects of it that formed the basis of my sceptical analysis:

The chief accuser in the case, Rev. Gribble, was unable to name a single informant for the rumours he reported that killings had occurred in the hinterland of Forrest River. Even the Commissioner found this strange.

The forensic evidence in the case – alleged human remains – was overwhelmingly negative.

The ballistics evidence – comprising a single bullet – was negative.

Many of those declared missing, presumed murdered had not been seen at the Mission or in the vicinity for anything betweenthree months and two years before being declared "missing" after the returnof the police patrol.

At least four of those declared missing are recorded as being at the Forrest River Mission in 1928, two years after their "murders".

One of the individuals on Gribble's list of the missing, allegedly murdered by the police, had in fact been killed in a tribal dispute by Aborigines three months before the police patrol left Wyndham.

The list could go on. Further, since the publication of *Massacre Myth*, I have found two other murder cases of the era that turned on forensic evidence that has a very important bearing on the Forrest River case. I hope to publish a paper on this matter in due course.

In addition, I have undertaken a detailed archival investigation of Rev. Gribble's role in two other Aboriginal cases of the 1920s in WA's far north. I believe the two monographs I have written on them clearly demonstrate his unreliability as a witness to the truth in a number of matters.

However, all this is logically and empirically distinct from the proposition that the story of Aboriginal dispossession in WA's far north, and elsewhere, is a deeply saddening one. Suffering occurred there and on other fronts of the colonial project as a result of, at times, violent depredations and social deprivations. Some academics, presumably trained for a far more intellectually rigorous approach to evidence, are increasingly conflating this very different proposition with claims concerning the Forrest River affair in particular.

A compassionate settlement and respectful relations with our fellow citizens of Aboriginal descent is surely supported by those guided by a good will. But it must all be based on the whole truth concerning the past.

Rod Moran

from Robert Manne

Late one night in November 1997 I made the mistake of speaking with Ron Brunton. I had heard that Brunton was writing a critique of Bringing them home. I told him I believed his talents would be better used in conducting his own research into Aboriginal child removal than in tearing Bringing them home apart. I told him, too, that, in my opinion, the kind of critique he proposed to publish would most likely to used by the Right to discredit the finding of Bringing them home and even to deny that over the question of the stolen generations a terrible injustice had occurred. Clearly Brunton was displeased. Since that late-night conversation, on at least half a dozen occasions, he has repeated in his articles and his lectures his faintly malicious version of what he claims I said.

I am surprised that Brunton thinks it ethical to speak in public about the subject matter of private conversation. Yet there is an even more important reason why partisan accounts of private conversations have no place in public disputes. In private conversation, most of us pull our punches and remain more or less polite, holding back from the kind of total candour the conduct of public controversy requires. When we spoke, I was, of course, aware of his track record as a spokesperson for the ideological Right in the area of Aboriginal affairs. When I said to Brunton that it would be better for everyone if he tried to throw new light on the policy of Aboriginal child removal by conducting his own research rather than by offering a critique of Bringing them home, I was not expressing a general hostility to some such critique but a suspicion that anything Brunton in particular was likely to write would be as one-sided and negative and carping as his earlier criticisms of the High Court's Mabo judgment or the Aboriginal Deaths in Custody Royal Commission had proved to be. What I also believed was that the kind of critique Brunton was likely to write would be used to deny the extremity of the injustices involved in the child removal policies and would, as a consequence, do considerable harm to some of the most powerless and vulnerable people in Australia. As it turned out, Brunton's report, Betraying the *Victims*, was in character and consequence more or less what I surmised it was likely to be.

At the beginning of his reply, Brunton claims that I 'apparently believe' that I can 'make reckless claims which are demonstrably false without being called to account'. I am at a loss to understand what he means. Brunton must know that the *Quarterly Essay* is a journal which actively solicits responses and that those I criticised in In Denial were personally invited by the editor of the *Quarterly Essay*, Peter Craven, to respond to what I had written. Brunton must also know that many of those I criticised in *In Denial* have columns in the major newspapers of Australia and that three either edit or have privileged access to the magazines *Quadrant*, *Adelaide Review* and *IPA Review*. Whatever does Brunton mean, that I thought I could say what I liked in In Denial without being 'called to account?'

If anything, since the publication of In Denial my problem has been to find a single member of the Right, in Sydney or Melbourne, who has been willing to engage in open debate about the stolen generations. In Melbourne I asked the manager of Readers' Feast bookshop to invite one of the anti-stolen generations campaigners, Andrew Bolt, to debate me at one of their regular forums. Bolt at first accepted, but then, for reasons that seemed to me quite spurious, suddenly pulled out. In Sydney the bookseller Bob Gould has invited a number of the local journalistic campaigners to debate me, thus far without result. As Brunton knows, I very readily agreed to a debate with him on the ABC's *7.30 Report*. His suggestion that I thought I could make 'reckless accusations' without being 'called to account' is simply preposterous.

Many of the criticisms contained in the early part of Brunton's reply – concerning my supposed moral vanity or desperation to extricate myself from association with the Right – are so *ad hominem* that there seems no point or indeed possibility of offering a dignified response. Concerning these slurs others must judge. All I can say to the charge of moral vanity is this. When I wrote in the past about the victims of communism rather than about Australian paternalism or racism towards Aborigines, no member of the Right seemed to think my books or essays were an expression of moral vanity.

Only one of Brunton's *ad hominem* attacks requires a detailed reply. Brunton points out, quite accurately, that in my early years as editor of *Quadrant* I received financial support from two of the mining companies that have also given support to the Institute of Public Affairs, for which he works. Am I implying, Brunton asks, that while I am 'too pure' to be tainted by such funding, the IPA is not?

This is not my implication at all. When I was editor of *Quadrant*, I opened the magazine to a debate on 'economic rationalism'. What I learned was that at least some of the financial support from the miners had, indeed, come with ideological strings attached. As a consequence, in my last four years as editor I did not approach any mining companies for support. Since writing In Denial I have discovered that Western Mining does not want Brunton on its advisory board and that, at least in part because of Brunton's reputation among Aboriginal groups, another major mining company has put an end to their financial support for the IPA. During the early 1990s, Brunton's work was of value to the mining companies in their political fight against native title. Since the mid-1990s the ideological work of the indigenous unit at the IPA and the economic interest of some of the mining companies, who have accepted the reality of native title and the need for amicable relations with local Aboriginal groups, have diverged. I accept that Brunton's work now, if anything, imperils the IPA's financial base.

At the centre of Brunton's reply is the claim that in In Denial I have grossly misrepresented him. Let us look at the three key instances of such supposed misrepresentation in turn.

Brunton claims that I slandered him when I argued that he, along with P.P. McGuinness, Christopher Pearson and Michael Duffy, argued that very many of the Aborigines who claim to have been separated from their mothers and families might be suffering from a condition known as 'false memory syndrome', an argument I regard as completely baseless, as deeply insulting to the victims of child removal and as, indeed, 'grotesque'.

It is undeniable that Ron Brunton was the first member of the anti-stolen generations campaign who suggested that 'false memory syndrome' might be an explanation for the stories the Aboriginal witnesses told the Wilson–Dodson inquiry. In Betraying the Victims, Brunton wrote: 'It is reasonable to ask for more detailed information [about the witnesses] ... particularly in the light of accumulating research pointing to the role of suggestion in creating false memories of events that never actually occurred.' The research to which Brunton was referring here was contained in an article which appeared in the Scientific American for September 1997. This article begins with the case of an American woman who 'became convinced that she had repressed memories of having been in a satanic cult, of eating babies, of being raped, of having sex with animals and being forced to watch the murder of her eight year old friend'.

Brunton now claims that he was merely concerned that others might think that the Aboriginal witnesses at the Wilson–Dodson inquiry were suffering from 'false memory syndrome'. This is a complete invention. In Betraying the Victims it was he who was so concerned.

The seed Brunton sowed in his suspicions about the possibility that Aboriginal witnesses might be suffering from the 'false memory syndrome', as described in *Scientific American*, fell on fertile ideological ground. In the following year, in *Quadrant*, P.P. McGuinness likened the testimony of the Aboriginal witnesses before the Wilson–Dodson inquiry to those who, in the grip of 'false memory syndrome', had invented tales of childhood sexual abuse, Satanic possession or alien abduction. Not long after McGuinness's intervention, another anti-stolen generations campaigner, Michael Duffy, informed the readers of the London *Spectator* about the 'brave commentator' who had compared stories of Aboriginal child removal 'with the failure of memory that occurs in other cases, such as people wrongly claiming childhood sexual assault or abduction by aliens'. Not only did Brunton not criticise McGuinness or Duffy for the use they made of his original suggestion. Instead Duffy's article was actually reprinted in the *IPA Review*, the magazine of the think-tank where Ron Brunton is employed as senior fellow in indigenous affairs. How I am meant to have slandered Brunton by pointing to him as the author of the 'false memory syndrome' canard or by associating him with fellow campaigners who took up his idea, one of whose article was reprinted in the house journal of the institute where he is employed, I must leave it to Brunton to explain.

And one final point. In Brunton's reply to In *Denial* he suggests that there is no fundamental difference between his claims about 'false memory syndrome' and my suggestion about the likelihood of many childhood memories being simplified or distorted with the passage of time. As Brunton writes: 'What he notes is just commonsense, but when I say something similar it is grotesque.' Once more Brunton is being quite disingenuous. In the Scientific American article to which he referred, it is made quite clear that 'false memory syndrome' is not about the distortion or simplification of memory of real events but the creation, by a process of suggestion, of memories of events that never occurred. In my view the claim, without even a shred of evidence, that the Aboriginal witnesses who appeared before the Wilson–Dodson inquiry might be suffering from a form of pathological fantasy is, indeed, as I wrote in In *Denial*, 'grotesque'.

Ron Brunton claims that I have also completely misrepresented him when I argued that he had criticised the Wilson–Dodson inquiry for its failure to ask for an extension of its terms of reference so that it could compare the situation of Aboriginal children separated from their parents and communities with the situation of separated non-Aboriginal children, or what he called, in the relevant section of *Betraying the Victims*, 'like with like'.

We have reached here the Talmudic moment in our exchange. Rather than engage in lengthy textual analysis of this section of *Betraying the Victims* and the range of his expression 'like with like' (the supposed core of my misrepresentation), let me quote instead from what Ron Brunton himself wrote on two occasions in the *Courier Mail* with reference to the only point of this dispute, namely whether or not I misrepresented him when I claimed that he believed that Aboriginal and non-Aboriginal child removals were phenomena of a fundamentally similar kind.

On 26 February 1998, Brunton wrote that *Bringing them home* 'wrongly denies the great similarities between the removal of Aboriginal children and government interference in the lives of children from poor and supposedly dysfunctional non-Aboriginal families'. The difference between 'great similarities' and 'like with like' is not apparent to me. In an article in the *Courier Mail* of 4 July 1998, Brunton was even more explicit. In this article Brunton compared the situation of the stolen generations, the situation of the 'child migrants' from Britain detailed in the television program *Lost Children of the Empire*, and the situation of illegitimate babies who were taken from their mothers and adopted out. He concluded in this article that:

> The three forms of child removal had much in common, despite attempts by 'stolen generations' advocates to minimise the similarities in order to sustain their absurd 'genocide' claim. All involved many cases where the authorities were callously indifferent to the human rights and feelings of the vulnerable and powerless people they were dealing with, and where laws were broken with impunity. Children were betrayed by those who were supposed to look after them. Many people had their lives shattered, both the children who were taken and the parents who lost them.

In this article not one point of dissimilarity between these three kinds of child removal is mentioned.

And yet Brunton now claims I have seriously misrepresented him by the simple claim that he regards the comparison of the removal of Aboriginal and non-Aboriginal children as a comparison of 'like with like'. If I have misunderstood Brunton, he has even more comprehensively misunderstood himself.

Ron Brunton also claims that I have seriously misrepresented him when I claim that he criticised *Bringing them home* for failing to include verbatim extracts from all the Aboriginal witnesses who appeared before the Wilson–Dodson inquiry. In *Betraying the Victims*, Brunton raises what he calls 'a disturbing possibility – that, for whatever reason, the Inquiry has not faithfully represented the evidence and submissions that were presented to it, and has given greater prominence to the negative accounts'. Later he writes: '... the report presents extracts from the confidential evidence of only 143 people ... But there has been very little attempt to provide summary information for the witnesses as a whole ... Consequently it seems fair to state that the experiences of the majority of witnesses have been largely ignored.'

My interpretation of this passage was that Brunton regarded the failure to quote directly from all the witnesses who had appeared before it as evidence that they had been 'largely ignored'. I was not the only reader of Brunton who came to this view. In the *Australian* Frank Devine argued: 'Brunton asserts that the evidence taken from 535 Aborigines was used selectively to paint the grimmest possible picture of suffering and injustice. Of the 143 people from whose testimony extracts were published ... only 14 of 250 quotations point to "anything like reasonably positive experiences" at any stage of life . . .' (*Australian* 5/3/98) Even more extraordinarily, Brunton himself wrote in the *Courier Mail* of 9 March 1998 that: 'The extracts from testimony included in the report came from less than 40 per cent of the witnesses, and it is therefore fair to say that the experiences of over 60 per cent were very largely ignored.' In *In Denial* I claimed that Brunton 'had accused the authors of *Bringing them home* of seriously and perhaps deliberately distorting the outcome of their inquiry because of the fact that of the 535 witnesses they heard, "only" 143 were quoted directly in their report'. In the *Courier Mail*, Brunton provides as his only evidence for the claim that 60 per cent of Aboriginal witnesses were 'very largely ignored' the fact that extracts from their testimony were not to be found in the text of *Bringing them home*. Once again it is not I who have misrepresented Brunton. It is Brunton who has misrepresented himself.

Brunton's self-misrepresentations do not end here. In *In Denial* I accused Brunton of disingenuousness. Brunton, I argued, had warned about those who might exploit the weaknesses of *Bringing them home* in order to deny that in the removal of Aboriginal children from their mothers and communities a terrible injustice had occurred. I pointed out that when, indeed, such voices were heard, Brunton did not criticise them. Rather he joined with them, on common platforms, as part of a political campaign. Brunton will have none of this. He claims that he is, indeed, a critic of the stolen generations denialists. He claims that sharing platforms with people such as P.P. McGuinness or Douglas Meagher is no evidence that he is involved with them in a common cause.

Both claims are false. It is true that on one occasion, his speech at the *Quadrant* conference in August 2000, Brunton devoted a few lines to denying that the stolen generations was an entire hoax along Hindmarsh Bridge lines. It is also true that in his large body of writings on the stolen generations that on one occasion, before the publication of In Denial, he distanced himself from the theory of the 'rescued' generations in a *single line*. However what is also undeniable is that throughout the political campaign against the stolen generations Brunton has been an enthusiastic participant with an essentially non-antagonistic relationship to all the major players. Let one example suffice. At the *Quadrant* 2000 conference, Brunton spoke after Douglas Meagher had offered the audience his unambiguous defence of the nobility of Aboriginal child removal. Not only did Brunton not criticise Meagher. Rather, he conceded humbly that, having listened to Meagher, he had been forced to recognise that 'I have only scratched the surface of *Bringing them home*'s mendacity.' It was at this conference that Brunton called publicly for the dismantling of the Human Rights and Equal Opportunities Commission. Of course, in theory sharing a common platform does not prove involvement in a common campaign. Yet anyone who has read or heard Brunton's contributions at the two *Quadrant* conferences would understand that his attendances involved enthusiastic participation in a common cause with people like Peter Howson, P.P. McGuinness, Keith Windschuttle and Douglas Meagher. Why does Brunton pretend that this was not the case?

The most important issue of contention between Brunton and myself concerns the issue of genocide and the stolen generations. In *In Denial* I argued against both *Bringing them home*'s claim about postwar assimilationist child removal as genocide but also against Ron Brunton's critique. My own position can be summarised like this. During the interwar years many Australian protectors and politicians, who believed it inevitable that eventually all tribal or 'full blood' Aborigines would die out, also became alarmed about the implications for Australia's future as a white society because of the rise in the numbers of the Aborigines they called 'half-castes'. Some of these protectors, most importantly A.O. Neville of Western Australia and Dr Cecil Cook of the Northern Territory, advanced eugenic arguments and policies whose purpose was to solve 'the problem of the half-caste' by a program called 'breeding out the colour', one of whose mechanisms was the separation of children from their families and communities. Both the Commonwealth government and the government of Western Australia supported these policies during the 1930s. I argued in *In Denial* that those who dreamt of an Aborigine-free Australia were thinking genocidally and that in the Commonwealth's support for Cook's implementation of the measures for 'breeding out the colour' and in the Western Australian government's sponsorship of A O Neville's 1936 legislation, which gave the native administrator additional child removal powers and the power to forbid all marriages between 'full bloods' and 'half-castes', genocidal thinking and administrative practice touched. I also argued that in the postwar period when the idea of biological absorption was abandoned in favour of sociocultural assimilation, the genocidal dimension in child removal policy came to an end.

After the publication of In Denial I hoped that Brunton, who had consistently treated the idea of genocide and the stolen generations as an outrage to commonsense, would do me the courtesy of a considered reply. It was not to be. Brunton can do no more than repeat his criticisms of Bringing them home on the genocide question, reveal yet again his incapacity to see the difference between birth control methods and policies designed to make a distinct people disappear, and return, yet again, to the fact that two Aboriginal activists in the 1930s published a manifesto which spoke in favour of biological absorption. Concerning the question of genocide and the stolen generations, it is now clear that Brunton is either unwilling or incapable of replying to the case both Raimond Gaita and I have, in slightly different ways, advanced.

When In Denial was published, Ron Brunton appeared to argue both on the 7.30 Report and in the Age that a Commonwealth government apology to the stolen generations and to the Aborigines in general was overdue. I must admit I was both puzzled at this development and pleased. On many previous occasions Brunton had sneered in print about the idea of an apology. When, for example, the draft declaration on reconciliation was released, he claimed that the deep confusion in the minds of the people who favoured an apology was itself 'good enough reason to view these demands with grave suspicion and to resist attempts to include such an apology in any reconciliation document'. (Courier Mail 12/6/99) On another occasion, after the Sydney Corroboree, Brunton mocked the 'caring and righteous people' who distinguished themselves from 'those other Australians, such as heartless John Howard and his legion of redneck supporters, who refuse to apologise to the "stolen generations"'.

When Brunton was reminded of statements like these, he strenuously denied he had had a change of heart. He had always, he said, been in favour of an apology. But of what kind? We should, he said he had always argued, apologise to the Aborigines for treating them as a different people. When deconstructed, what this meant was that we should apologise, equally, for depriving Aborigines of the vote or incarcerating them on reserves before the 1960s and for granting them land rights with inalienable title or recognising their unique status in the succeeding years. Brunton is, then, and has always been, in favour of an apology. It is the kind of apology John Howard and, as Raimond Gaita commented, even Pauline Hanson would find easy to make. It is also the kind of apology almost no Aborigine could accept. What kind of person is it who thinks it appropriate to offer an apology to a group in such a form that almost all of those to whom the apology is offered would think that they had been offered a deliberate insult? With Ron Brunton, on the issue of the apology to the stolen generations and on much else besides, it is always vital to read the fine print.

II

I am puzzled that someone who is usually so perceptive a writer as Inga Clendinnen and so attentive a reader should have made so many obvious mistakes in her comments about In Denial. Let me try to clear the decks of these matters as swiftly as possible so that I can get to what is genuinely at the core of our disagreement.

Clendinnen argues that since my first essay on the stolen generations, which was delivered as the Stephen Murray-Smith Lecture in November 1997, my 'attitude to the critics' of Bringing them home has 'hardened'. A moment's reflection would have allowed Clendinnen to see that this is not so. In November 1997 there were no published criticisms of Bringing them home. If Clendinnen looks again she will discover that every book and article analysed in In Denial was published after the Murray-Smith Lecture was delivered, not before. It is not my attitude that has hardened. It is, rather, that in November 1997 the campaign to undermine the credibility of Bringing them home had not yet begun.

Clendinnen argues that in In Denial I claimed that 'all the people who have clustered around Quadrant in the last three years "have moved from the promise of 'genuine debate' on Aboriginal policy to the reality of atrocity denialism in the David Irving mode".' I make no such claim. If Inga Clendinnen reads the relevant passage again she will discover that when I write of 'denialism in the David Irving mode', I am referring exclusively to the contribution of Keith Windschuttle in his three-part Quadrant series 'The Myths of Frontier Massacres'. Although he is of course dealing with killings on a vastly smaller scale, like Irving concerning Jewish deaths in the Holocaust, Windschuttle's purpose in this article is to claim, on the basis of little grasp of the relevant historical scholarship, that the numbers of Aborigines killed on the frontier have been largely inflated for a sinister political purpose – namely, Aboriginal 'separatism' and the 'break up' of the Australian state. In In Denial I do not apply the idea of Irving-style revisionism to any other participant or fellow traveller in the anti-stolen generations campaign, although in his unevidenced assertion that stories concerning the poisoning of Aborigines can best be regarded as a rural version of the urban myth, the publisher of Windschuttle, P.P. McGuinness, is certainly a serious contender for a description of such a kind.

Clendinnen is made 'nervous' by my claim that it is quite false to argue that in the interwar period in Australia the motives of those who removed 'half-caste' children from their mothers were of a 'social welfarist kind'. She thinks that I have argued that their motives were based more or less exclusively on the desire to keep Australia white. In fact my argument is more complicated than this. Some of the protectors were, certainly, concerned about the danger to White Australia of the growing 'half-caste' numbers. However, what I argue in In Denial, on the basis of archival research, is that in the interwar period the most important reason for removing 'half-caste' Aboriginal children from their mothers and communities was to rescue these 'half-European' children from the supposedly dirty and degraded condition of a life among barbarous, heathen tribal Aborigines. If concerns about malnutrition or neglect had been the motive for child removals in the interwar period, as many Australians (including Paul Kelly) still believe, why was there virtually no single case where a 'full-blood' child was removed? It was only in the assimilation period of the 1950s and 1960s that social welfare motives of a more recognisable kind began to play an important part in Aboriginal child removal practices, although even now such motives were so permeated with racial thinking that the twin elements – social welfarism and racism – are often almost impossible to separate. In In Denial I hoped that the story of Malcolm Charles Smith might illuminate this point.

Inga Clendinnen thinks I am blind to the genuinely 'good intentions' of many of those who separated the Aboriginal children or who, subsequently, looked after them in special-purpose institutions where they grew up. Indeed she believes I need a lesson in moral complexity and in the real-world interrelationship between intentions and outcomes which, courtesy of Gitta Sereny, she supplies with the story (rather confusing in the context) about the Nazi child removal policies concerning Aryan-looking Poles. In fact, in In Denial I spoke directly of one of the paradoxes of this episode in our history by reference to the case of people like Sister Kate Clutterbuck or Sister Eileen Heath, who were both saintly in the way they cared for the separated Aboriginal children but also incapable, in the way they thought about 'the problem of the half-caste' or the justifications they gave for the removals, of emancipating themselves from what I called 'the prevailing racist ways of thought'. In the end, moreover, I believe, like Robert van Krieken, that the intentions of those involved in child removal are less important than the institutional settings, the racial mindset and the supporting laws.

Like many others, including Ron Brunton in his reply, Inga Clendinnen thinks that in In Denial I have argued for the existence of a 'conspiracy' involving Quadrant magazine, the Howard Government and 'some of the bigger players in mining and other ventures'. I have made no such claim. Political conspiracies take place in secret. The political campaign against Bringing them home, which involved some people who are close political friends and some people who, I assume, had never heard of each other until the campaign gained momentum, was nothing if not open. The only participants in this campaign whose involvement proceeded more through winks and nudges than overt support were members of the Howard Government, in particular the Prime Minister and his Minister for Aboriginal Affairs, Senator John Herron.

In my argument, the government's support for the anti-stolen generations campaign was shown by the nature of the brief given to Commonwealth counsel in the Cubillo–Gunner case in Darwin and in the way details from the transcript of evidence in the case were leaked to friendly journalists at strategic moments of the trial. In my view, John Howard's support for the campaign was indicated by his willingness to relaunch Quadrant on its return from Melbourne to Sydney, and John Herron's by his speech at Quadrant's first conference on the Aborigines in 1999. Any lingering doubts about their involvement in the campaign were dispelled when, at the conclusion of my writing of In Denial, the Prime Minister called Andrew Bolt's disgraceful 'I Wasn't Stolen' attack on Lowitja O'Donoghue 'highly significant' and when, after his retirement, Senator Herron instantly associated himself with many of the most prominent anti-stolen generations campaigners by becoming President of the assimilationist Bennelong Society with Peter Howson as Vice President and Ray Evans of Western Mining, whose role as the éminence noire of the Right in Australia I discussed in In Denial, as Secretary.

The overwhelmingly most important issue for Inga Clendinnen raised by In Denial is my discussion of the relationship between the practice of Aboriginal child removal and the concept of genocide. Clendinnen seems to think that between the Murray-Smith lecture and In Denial my attitude on genocide, rather like my attitude to the critics of Bringing them home, has hardened. Again, this is not the case. If anything, the opposite is true. In In Denial I make it clearer than I did in 1997 that while certain administrators in the 1930s, in their plans to 'breed out' the 'half-castes' and in their imagining of an Australia that was Aborigine-free, were thinking in a genocidal way, at the very most can it be said of this period of history that genocidal thinking and administrative policy 'briefly touched'. I also made it clearer in In Denial than I did in 1997 why I disagree with the conclusion of Bringing them home that in the postwar assimilation period child removal involved the crime of genocide. Because, of course, I understand how difficult and sensitive the idea of genocide is, I can assure Inga Clendinnen that I still regard such discussions as the kind where people of good will ought to be able, with mutual respect, to disagree.

Clendinnen thinks that the discussion of genocide and Aboriginal child removal is 'a moral, intellectual and ... political disaster'. I will leave the question of politics to one side, except for a brief observation – namely that if the case about the relationship of Aboriginal child removal to genocidal thinking is true, the failure to discuss it seriously, because of a concern about the political consequences, would be, in my opinion, not only unprincipled but also cowardly. (I say cowardly because on no other question in my adult life, which has not been free of controversy, have I been subjected to more sustained abuse than over the discussion of genocide and the stolen generations.)

Let me turn to the moral and intellectual dimensions of this issue. Perhaps the deepest problem with the concept of genocide is the way it has come to be regarded almost as synonym for the Holocaust. With Inga Clendinnen this is clearly the case. She tells us that when she hears the word genocide she sees in her mind pictures of the Nazi war on the Jews and gypsies and, at a stretch, of Armenians in the First World War being driven to their deaths by the Turks. Although this is all understandable, it does not help rational debate. If Inga Clendinnen were to refer to the relevant academic literature on genocide, she would discover that most of those who have thought hard about the concept move further afield, and especially to the many instances of what they call colonial genocide. She would also discover that far from being 'mirror-bright', the concept of genocide is often bafflingly complex and opaque.

One difficulty is this. Because of its intimate association in the public mind with the Holocaust, the concept of genocide has embedded within it two rather different kinds of meaning. Because of the murderous means used by the Nazis to exterminate the Jews, for very many people genocide has become another word for massive political killing by the state. Such people would agree with Clendinnen that to take 'murder out of genocide' is to render the concept 'vacuous'. Because, however, of the ambition of the Nazis in the Holocaust, to rid the earth of the Jews, for many writers, including Hannah Arendt and Zygmunt Bauman, it is not killing which is at the core of the concept of genocide but the desire and the decision to weed from the garden of humankind a people deemed by others not fit to live. Raimond Gaita's idea about the elimination of a distinct people through a program of sterilisation is an attempt to illuminate this way of thinking about genocide for those who regard genocide as merely another word for mass state killing.

The argument concerning genocide and the stolen generations that I have tried to make, time and again, rests on this second understanding of genocide. The argument can be expressed like this. If it is true that some interwar administrators genuinely believed that 'full-blood' tribal Aborigines could not survive contact with higher European civilisation; and if, at the same time, they believed that the remaining 'half-castes' could be absorbed biologically in the space of four or five generations by a eugenics policy, including child removal, supported by the state; and if, in addition, they believed that Australia would be a better society if in fifty or a hundred years no people would be alive who thought of themselves as Aboriginal – then I think it accurate to speak of these thoughts and the policies to implement them as genocidal in character and intent.

Clendinnen believes that the 'rascals' who became involved in the anti-Bringing them home campaign only became so involved because their minds shut down when they heard the word genocide. I do not think this is true. As Martin Krygier has pointed out in a letter to the *Australian's Review of Books*, Sir William Deane, who has never endorsed the idea of genocide against the stolen generations, has been subjected to the same kind of derision from the Right, because of his speeches about Aboriginal injustice and Australian history, as has Sir Ronald Wilson. Nor do I think the word 'rascals' – in common understanding impish, naughty boys – is remotely adequate as a description of those who have argued, for example, that the Aboriginal people whose lives have been blighted by removal from their mothers and communities might be suffering from 'false memory syndrome' or that they ought to feel grateful to those who 'rescued' them from ostracism within Aboriginal society or even something worse.

Clendinnen tells us that she does not like 'adversarial' history of the kind she thinks I have written in *In Denial*. What she likes or dislikes is, of course, no business of mine. However I think she should recognise that questions of style are not mere matters of taste. In matters of intellectual dispute, or so it seems to me, while clarity and accuracy are of greatest importance, the tone adopted ought to fit the case. Intolerance concerning genuine points of disagreement is never justifiable, but neither is an indifferent-seeming coolness in the face of blindness to the suffering of others. Sometimes an adversarial style is inappropriate. Sometimes it is not.

Clendinnen sees in my writing a decline from the admirable Orwellian coolness of *The Culture of Forgetting* to the regrettable Blakean passion of *In Denial*. Others must judge if she is right. In my defence all I wish to say is that it was the combination of precision and passion that first attracted me to the political essays of George Orwell, who is always a fierce adversarialist, and that there is no political poem that stirs me more deeply than William Blake's 'Jerusalem'. Indeed it was Orwell, above all other writers, who convinced me that when I wrote about the kinds of political issues that interested me most deeply – questions of justice – the sword should not sleep in my hand.

III

Michael Duffy writes: 'Robert Manne's claim that criticisms of parts of the Bringing them home report represent "an attempt to deny ... that a really terrible injustice occurred" is wrong. Anyone who has read my columns in the Courier Mail or the Daily Telegraph will be aware how he has misrepresented them to reach such an insulting conclusion.'

Duffy's comment is, in my opinion, truly breathtaking in its dishonesty. As, however, every time I paraphrase or summarise Duffy he claims to be misrepresented (on the knowledge that virtually no one will check for themselves), I have decided to quote verbatim the relevant passage from an article on the stolen generations which Duffy wrote for the London Spectator (15/4/00) and which was reprinted in the IPA Review (July 2000). I will leave it to readers to decide for themselves whether I have misrepresented Michael Duffy or whether he has misrepresented himself.

> In the first 60 or so years of the twentieth century, some mainly part-Aboriginal children were separated from their parents and in most cases brought up in church institutions or boarding schools. 'Bringing Them Home', the report of a government inquiry in the 1990s, found that this occurred to between 10 and 30 per cent of all Aborigines, and that the predominant motivation was racial assimilation. It concluded that, as the ultimate purpose was to 'breed out the colour' and destroy the Aboriginal race (it was assumed full-bloods would die off anyway), the practice amounted to genocide. This inquiry received an enormous amount of publicity and, building on other concerns about Aboriginal well-being, has created an atmosphere of enthusiastic shame surrounding the public discussion of Aboriginal issues.
>
> The problem is that there appears to be little truth in almost any of this. The inquiry's attempts to identify how many children were separated were futile, but 10 per cent was probably the top of the range rather than the bottom. (This is the figure provided by the

Australian Bureau of Statistics.) The inquiry did not interview any of the officials involved in the separations. They have subsequently come forward and helped establish that the motivation of the separations was often welfare, not racial assimilation. For instance, some tribes in the late 1940s refused to accept some of the children born of liaisons between black women and Australian or American servicemen during the war. So their mothers asked the welfare people to take the children to church homes to be brought up.

Mothers asked the white authorities to look after their children in many other circumstances, too. Charles Perkins is the most famous black activist in Australia. He was heard recently on the BBC predicting that Sydney would burn during Aboriginal protests at the time of the Olympic Games. He is often portrayed as a stolen child, but in fact his mother asked that he be sent from the outback to a boarding school in the city to get a good education (just as white children in the same circumstances were also sent).

Another example of the elusive nature of the 'stolen generations' lies with two of the most tragic stories told in the government inquiry's report. In each case the person involved is suing the government. The cases are not yet finished, but evidence to date indicates that neither was in fact 'stolen'. One brave commentator has compared this with the failure of memory that occurs in other cases, such as people wrongly claiming childhood sexual assault or abduction by aliens.

It is a commonplace in the press that 100,000 children were wrenched from their mothers' arms, and that 'no black family' was untouched by this attempted genocide. The effects of such claims on the feelings of white (and indeed black) Australia can be imagined, yet they are gross exaggerations. Although no-one knows, it's possible the number really 'stolen' against their parents' will was as low as several thousand.

Unfortunately, this enthusiastic embrace of falsehood and delusion by many white Australians is typical of their approach to Aboriginal matters.

Is there any word in the above that shows recognition that in the policies and practices of Aboriginal child removal a terrible injustice occurred?

IV

I am sorry to disappoint Rod Moran in regarding Neville Green's textured history of the Forrest River massacres and Aboriginal oral accounts as more persuasive than the case for the defence he has mounted in *Massacre Myth*. All I wish to reiterate is that others will in the end have to determine where the truth lies by the normal means of historical argument. I am content with Moran's agreement that the ultimate decision of the historians on the question of Forrest River will not justify what I believe is the way Windschuttle has attempted to use his book – namely to buttress his general position, that stories about frontier massacres are, more often that not, merely 'myths'.